Kung Fu Theology

A practical journey of how

to contend for the faith

*Keep fighting for the faith
and loving Jesus!
Steve Allen*

S<small>TEVE</small> A<small>LLEN</small>

Kung Fu Theology

Trade Paperback ISBN 979-8-9876371-1-1

eBook ISBN 979-8-9876371-0-4

Special thanks to www.Word-2-Kindle.com for their help in formatting and cover design and their partnership.

Printed in the United States of America
2023

For more information regarding Kung Fu Theology, the author, speaking engagements, coaching, or individualized instruction, please go to www.kungfutheology.com.

To Carrie,
My partner in marriage, in raising
kids, and in ministry

Contents

Introduction

"I wish I could have more impact."

"I wish I had a deeper understanding of the person of Christ and what He has called me to." It's comments like these that I have heard over the years, and still do today as people are searching for greater authenticity in their own faith, and a greater impact on the world around them. As I have personally wrestled with both of these ideas, through my journeys around the world from the Far East to the Middle East to Eastern Washington, I have encountered many people who live out answers to both of the preceding desires. And this is my effort to put into words those characteristics that seem to be present in those who are living out faith and have a deeply intimate relationship with Christ and see long-lasting fruit as a result.

My story is not necessarily much different than any of yours. I grew up in Eastern Washington, married my high school sweetheart, and became a high school English teacher. But through our early years of learning how to do ministry, our desire to start a family, and through the influence of a lot of people, I began to see my own heart change as I started to understand more and more what it meant to be a follower of Christ and not just a spectator. After having two biological children, we adopted three girls from China, and then we made the big jump from leaving a teaching job that I loved to pursue full-time vocational ministry. It was during these seasons was when I found my desires changing from praying about what God wanted for my life, to what God wanted from my life. Though the process continues today, I walk in greater conviction that my life is not my own and I must learn to surrender more and more as I pursue Christ.

Being a former English teacher, I have always been intrigued with metaphors, and having spent a significant amount of time in China, I am also intrigued by their culture. I first heard Bruce Lee's quote about becoming like water shortly after I stood in front of his statue at the edge of Hong Kong's Victoria Harbor. It immediately made an impression upon me which was where the creation of the idea of Kung Fu Theology originated. I knew there was a deep Biblical truth that God was revealing to me as a result. I have seen redemptive analogies all around the world that reveal these Biblical truths, and for me, this was another one. This was similar to watching the Dai Water Festival in southwest China of people splashing water to rid themselves of the mistakes and evil of the past year. This book is not about elevating Bruce Lee or Eastern ideology; it is about pointing people to Jesus and the importance of becoming like water in how we minister, or better yet, how Paul said it: "Become all things to all people so that by all possible means I might save some."

It is my hope that this book will be a catalyst to connecting you more intimately to the person of Jesus, and inspire you to let God write your story which will be littered with moments where others get to know the salvation and grace of our Lord, Jesus Christ.

Enjoy the journey through these pages as you hear real narratives and Biblical truth and discover how Kung Fu Theology will change how you live. And may Jesus be glorified in your journey.

Part 1

Solid Theology

CHAPTER 1

Kung Fu Theology

When you reach the edge of the Jordan's waters, go and stand in the river. Joshua 3:8

"I have but one passion: it is He, it is He alone. The world is the field and the field is the world; and henceforth that country shall be my home where I can be most used in winning souls for Christ." Nicolaus Ludwig von Zinzendorf

Stepping out of the van, the pungent aroma of jasmine met me before my foot hit the ground. Midmorning, even here in the village, the tea was always hot and the persimmons were piled high. We hadn't driven too far from the city but as I looked around me, it felt like we had traveled centuries. The one-room brick houses were each missing a pane or two of glass from the single, small window, the tiny garden plot was green and ripe for the evening noodles, and the bricks forming the walls looked like they were each made by hand due to their irregularities. Anshan is the steel capital of China and home to millions of laborers, but here in this nearby village it was simple. So simple it was appealing. Each home consisted of a concrete platform that was a sofa in the daytime and heated by cornstalks at night for the entire family to sleep. A small hotplate sat in the corner with a wok nearby, and a small dresser held two or three changes of clothing. That's it. No computers, or televisions, or cellphones, or appliances, or cars, or any other necessity I had back at home—just a few people doing life together.

During my week in Anshan, I still had not seen a single foreigner. Black hair filled the sidewalks and dotted the distance. But I wasn't there for business. Well, not economic business. I was there for kingdom business. We were there to help the poorest of the poor who had chosen to keep their disabled children. These people struck my heartstrings as I have three healthy daughters from China whose parents chose not to keep them for probably a myriad of reasons. And mine were healthy girls. The children I saw in these villages were mostly plagued with CP. A few were unable to walk and sat in wheelchairs that the local thrift shop back home would probably decline taking. Each family we met had a story and it felt like we were trading our bags of rice and fruit, and a jar of oil for the telling of it. Strangely, they weren't stories of sadness. They were stories of obstacles.

The house we stopped in front of looked like all of the others. A small garden greeted us and welcomed me as possibly the first foreigner it had ever met. In front of the door that was barely hanging on the hinges sat a boy about the age of my son, maybe nine, who was confined to a wheelchair. He smiled as we drew near and his grandparents lit up when they saw our armfuls of supplies. I never saw any parents there, but grandparents caring for children was a common sight. And this set of grandparents looked like they walked out of an antique photo album. He wore a Mao jacket and hat. His face was weathered, but there was still a glint in his eyes. In his right hand he held a pipe and in his left was his garden hoe. He wasn't tall, but he also wasn't short. He was just typical. The grandmother though stood out. As soon as we drew near, she started chattering with our host. I don't know a lot of Mandarin but I did know the word *laowai*, and *gao*, and *da bizi*. I guess being called a tall, big-nosed foreigner wasn't supposed to be insensitive, and for me it wasn't. I know that I am all three of those—especially in China. The grandmother was a hoot though. She scurried around pouring tea and gathering a small bowl of peanuts. I guess she was like most grandmas— guests arrive and she gets to work. There was something sweet though in how she stroked her grandson's hair and smiled in his eyes. Her smile was what drew my interest. Her toothless grin lit up her aging skin that had obviously seen a lot of sunny days in the village. It was clear that this boy was loved.

After distributing gifts, my host talked passionately with the family for the next twenty minutes. I picked up a bit about the boy's health, and his education but that was about it. As is often the case, the conversation closed abruptly. My host asked if I would pray for the family while he translated. And so I did. I prayed what you would expect—healing, provision, peace, and God's favor. As we opened our eyes, the grandmother looked at me and spoke a small simple sentence, *"Wo jiang yao jian li yi ge jiao hui"*—I'm starting a church. I looked at my host and asked him, "Is she starting a church?" Xu, my host, nodded his head. I looked back at the grandmother and said a single word that probably revealed more about my theology than about her faith: "How?" From my experience, I knew how we started churches back home. A group would be sent, a building found, singers would audition, and chairs would be bought. She only said a few sentences to Xu who told me, "There are a group of women in this village and they meet at the banyan tree most days. They have one Bible. She doesn't know how to read so another woman reads the Bible. Then whatever the Bible says to do, they do it." That was it. It was so simple, yet so pure. As we climbed into the van, I kept thinking about those words from an illiterate, poor, toothless grandmother who understood more about scripture than I did in my forty years of following Jesus, running youth groups, pastoring a church, and leading my family. "Whatever it says to do, we do it."

I wish that was my theology. I wish it was how I studied the Bible. But it wasn't. It was many years ago that I heard that line and I'm still challenged by whether or not I follow that way of thinking. I like to think that I do. I want to say I that do. But I find myself following the Jeffersonian Bible where I just pick and choose the parts I want to include and leave out the tough pieces or the parts that create conflict with my comfortable way of life. It's this comfortable life that I'm surrounded with—warm houses, deep retirement accounts, multiple cars, secure jobs, and every need met that defines the people of Eastern Washington. In fact, it defines most areas of the U.S.

I remember riding the high-speed train back to Beijing from Anshan. The trip is dotted with farmland. As a foreigner who lives near wheat fields, this farmland was so different. Each plot of land was a football field-sized lot, had a yak, and a dilapidated old farmhouse. The pictures I would see online of centuries-old farmers are the same photos that I could have taken—the bamboo hat, the rickety old bicycle, and the wife working the sickle while the husband drove the plow. From a missiological view though, this is where the simplicity of the rural life became complex. In China, with nearly 1.5 billion people and only a hundred thousand Christ followers, how does the Gospel spread in a restricted access nation? It happens one person at a time. But that's the beauty of the Gospel movement in China; it has happened in the midst of persecution and strict oversight. It happened from one beggar telling another where there was bread. It comes from one life intersecting with another on their terms, in their world.

Something significant happened that day for me in the village that was formative in learning how to minister. In reading the Bible that I thought was detached from contemporary methodology, I learned that God's word is as alive today as it ever was. Paul wrote in 1 Corinthians 9:20-23,

> "To the Jews I became like a Jew, to win the Jews. To those under the law I became like one under the law (though I myself am not under the law), so as to win those under the law. To those not having the law I became one not having the law (although I am not free from God's law but am under Christ's law). So as to win those not having the law. To the weak I became weak, to win the weak. I have become all things to all men so that by

all possible means I might save some. I do all
this for the sake of the Gospel, that I might
share in its blessing."

His words still echo in my mind as I think of that
warm afternoon standing in front of the broken down
home. Paul knew. His words, "I have become all things
to all men so that by all possible means I might save
some," may be the one verse in the Bible that best
captures the methodology of sharing Christ. This call
to share Christ is obvious just by looking at the last
words that Jesus spoke in each of the Gospels:

In Matthew 28:19, Jesus says, "Therefore go and
make disciples of all nations."

In Mark 16:15, Jesus says, "Go into all the world
and preach the gospel to all creation."

In Luke 24:17, Jesus says, "Repentance for the
forgiveness of sins will be preached in his name to
all nations." In each of these, Scripture is clear in the
command to go, but finding the methodology behind
it is not. But Paul gives a command that withstands
time and culture and reminds people from every location how to minister best: "I became all things to all
people so that I might win some." Paul is not saying that we should compromise Biblical principles or
commands to share with people, but he is saying that
you need to be able to engage people in the marketplace and in a way that is culturally relevant to them,

on their terms, and in their space. This is difficult for most Christians because we tend to operate out of what we know and what is safe.

When I was teaching high school English, each of my student teachers would do the same thing during their first lesson—they would lecture. When pressed as to why, the common answer was, "That's the way I was taught." The Western church is not much different—church is on Sunday mornings, probably at 10:00, three songs are sung with announcements and an offering sprinkled in someplace, and then the pastor will give a thirty-two minute sermon with 3-5 points. But is this the most effective way to introduce people to the King of Kings?

A visible way to demonstrate Paul's teaching is to hold out both of your hands—your right being clenched in a fist, your left laying open palm up. In the right is your doctrine. Hang on to that tightly as it is uncompromising and inflexible. Nothing changes it. But in your left is your methodology. You hold it with an open hand because it is changing with the culture. If you hold them both loosely with open hands, you become a liberal; if you clench them both, you become a fundamentalist. Instead, one you hold tightly, and the other you hold loosely.

And this is where Kung Fu Theology sets in. It looks at the methodology of ministering in a post-modern culture. Bruce Lee, perhaps the face of all martial arts, made his famous statement—one that can be redeemed for reaching people for Christ. It has a principle in it that is critical for moving people to minister in the world. Lee said,

> "Empty your mind, be formless, shapeless— like water. Now you put water into a cup, it becomes the cup; you put water into a bottle, it becomes the bottle; you put it into a teapot, it becomes the teapot. Now water can flow or it can crash. Be water my friend."[1]

Sounds similar to what Paul said in 1 Corinthians 9:22, "To the weak I became weak, to win the weak. I have become all things to all men so that by all possible means I might save some. I do all this for the sake of the Gospel, that I may share in its blessings."

Be water. Bruce Lee has it right. When ministering to people today, as Paul said, we are to become all things—to reach people right where they are, just as Jesus did. Jesus was in the marketplace, he met with the prostitutes, he met with the tax collectors, he met with the sick. He was like water—not constrained by customs or context, but modeling ministry in a real way that we may have forgotten. So often, we expect people to come to our church, conform to our customs, adopt our behaviors, and try to fit them into a paradigm that they are unfamiliar with or just plain not interested in at the time. But that is not the way Jesus operated. The church today is so quick to adopt Jesus' mission and message, but they often forget to adopt his methods too. This methodology is seen in Luke 19:

> "Jesus entered Jericho and was passing through. A man was there by the name of Zacchaeus; he was a chief tax collector and was wealthy. He wanted to see who Jesus was, but because he was short he could not see over the crowd. So he ran ahead and climbed a sycamore fig tree to see him, since Jesus was coming that way. When Jesus reached the spot, he looked up and said to him, 'Zacchaeus, come down immediately. I must stay at your house today.' So he came down at once and welcomed him gladly. All the people saw this and began to mutter, 'He has gone to be the guest of a sinner.'"[2]

Think for a moment about Jesus' methods—he went to the home of someone who may be the most despised person in the community. He probably shared a meal, visited, and received whatever hospitality was given to him. But he crossed all sorts of invisible barriers in doing so. And that's what liquid methodology looks like. Jesus is able to transcend these barriers because he is not defined by the culture or expectations or societal patterns that are restrictive and would keep most of us out of Zaccheus's house. This seems to be where the western mindset of Christianity has broken down. The attractional model of church has become the obstacle. Rather than becoming all things to all people, instead we just try to get people to a church service on a Sunday morning. We have relinquished our job of loving people and sharing the gospel to paid professionals on the stage who may not even be able to put a name to the face.

I've ministered as far away as Fort Portal, Uganda, to Alexandria, Egypt, to Wroclaw, Poland, to Heredia, Costa Rica; no one, not the hidden house church Chinese pastor in Li Jiang, nor the worker in the slums of Manila, demonstrates better the implementation of Kung Fu Theology than one single, solitary woman I met in Nicaragua.

Let me tell you a story. Like most January days in Managua, the heat hung in the late morning ready to devour its afternoon sojourners. We had been in a nearby village for a few days helping homeless families transplant onto permanent land with a permanent home. As we moved back to the city, I had asked about going to the La Chureca dump, which I had read about in preparation of our trip. Our host made a simple reply to my request, "You must have a police escort." Whether it was the adventurer inside of me or my lack of discretion in assessing the dangers, I quickly inquired about how we could get one. A day later the ten of us were on our simple bus heading to the dump. I don't know if anyone else on our team was too excited about the trip, for all they heard was the word, dump.

They didn't know 2,000 people lived there, many of them second and third generation families. We turned the corner into the dump and it may have been the most profound, most toxic place I had ever seen. As I looked out the front window of the bus, mountains and mountains of garbage were piled high as far as the eye cold see. Vultures dug through the garbage and circled overhead looking for any decaying flesh. And the breeze...oh, the breeze...which just an hour ago had brought a slight respite to a warm morning, was now blowing in fumes that verged somewhere near what death must smell like at the bottom of some drain.

Scanning to the left, a roughhewn cart pulled by an aged donkey had two kids on it who couldn't have been more than eight. One was barefoot and the other seemed to be wearing clothes she probably found that morning. They would jump out every time they saw a plastic bottle or anything of value and added it to the bags on the back of the cart. They were oblivious to the bus load of foreigners but apparently knew that in order to eat tomorrow, they must work today. An armed policeman pulled up interrupting our disbelief of what was in front of us. Fortunately, he knew some

English. After a few pleasantries, I asked him if there was anything good happening in the dump. His face lit up and he nearly shouted his reply, "Oh, you must meet Pastor Maria!" We quickly piled into the back of his truck and left our waiting bus.

You know those times that it feels like you are either in the middle of a dream or a movie? Well, this was one of those times. We drove through the dump past sunken-eyed men and women sniffing glue, some searching for food, and others just sitting. And the garbage just went on and on like a labyrinth where no one could escape. Then a solitary building appeared on a slight bluff. As the truck stopped, we all jumped out, and out walked a four-foot-nothing woman in her late forties who looked nothing like the women we just passed. She almost glowed with joy even as she began to tell us her story.

"I was a single mom working as a seamstress making a few cordobas a day for my little girl. One night at my home, which is just past the edge of the dump, I walked into the kitchen and heard God say to me, "Maria, I want you to go to La Chureca and preach the Gospel."

There was a slight grin on her face as she told the next part, which I think shocked all of us.

"No, Lord," I told Him. I went back into the living room and resolved to avoid the kitchen the rest of the night since that is where God was speaking.

In my mind, I could picture Moses doing the same thing with the burning bush, or Abraham at Moriah. It seemed so wrong, yet seemed so real as I knew I may do the same thing if God called me to go to an area that seemed far from Him.

I sat in my living room for awhile and then finally went back into the kitchen thinking God had left to ask some other willing soul. But when I got there, I knew God was waiting for me. "Maria, I want you to go to La Chureca and preach the Gospel." I didn't want to say yes, but I did and so I went to my pastor to see what he thought I should do and how I should proceed. When I met with him the next day, all he said was, "Maria, you can't go. They'll kill you there." So I went. I didn't know what to do or how to start as I am just an uneducated seamstress.

By this time, she had all of us enraptured into her story and anxiously waiting to hear more. We all ignored the stench and heat around us knowing we had just entered a tale that we would tell for years to come. Maria pointed to the ground right where we were standing outside this cinderblock, tin-roofed building and proceeded on.

Right there. Right where you are standing. I didn't know what to do but I knew God told me to preach the Gospel. So I put a milk crate down on the ground, stood on it, and just starting reading the book of John. It didn't take long until people started coming to hear what this little woman was saying. They gathered one by one, and then by three's and four's. Eventually as I looked in the distance, all across the dump, I could see lanterns moving my direction in the dusk sky— prostitutes, drug dealers, criminals, the marginalized all gathering around this little sewing lady that God told to go. As I continued reading, I could see tears streaming down many of their faces. "Why are you crying?" I asked them.

And then she said words that I would never forget: *No one ever told us there was a God who loved us.*

I'm not sure what all she said after that. It was just those words, "No one ever told us." It was just that simple. It was Kung Fu Theology. It was Paul becoming all things to all people so that he might win some. It wasn't a program; it wasn't committees. It was just the rawness of one person saying yes. Maria wasn't qualified. She hadn't created a 5-year strategic plan. She just heard the call and went. Abram went to an unknown land. Joshua stepped into the river. David picked up a stone. Peter cast his net. And Maria went to the dump.

That day, Maria went on and told us about the church she planted in the dump, about the hundreds of people who have come to faith, about the dignity people found, and how that church is now reaching out to others.

Over the next pages of this book, you are going to meet real people—ordinary people who are liquefying. I've met each of them and honestly, they aren't anything special in human terms. They are mechanics, moms, small business owners, farmers. Just ordinary people serving an extraordinary God. The common denominator is that they are all people who have become like water to reach those around them so that they might win some.

And this is where you step into the story. A man who two thousand years ago invited you into the story he is writing throughout time to find those who seem farthest away and introduce them to the Giver of Life. As we move through these chapters, you'll hear about more Marias and more Chinese grandmas, but I want to encourage you to not get lost in these stories, but to see under the waterline into how God moves people, and how he may be calling you. There's a principle in this idea of Kung Fu Theology that I don't want you to miss. I'm fully aware that Bruce Lee didn't follow Christian ideology. That many of you may say this blurs the lines of accepting false religious belief. But I think, with many things, we have the option to receive them, reject them, or redeem them. Do we receive it as it is? Reject it entirely? Or see how it might be redeemed to reinforce a Biblical principle and give a perspective that might help people understand it better and put it into practice. Or as James says, "Do not merely listen to the word, and so deceive yourselves. Do what it says."[3]

Come take the journey of how to hold theology tightly and methodology loosely. We are going to begin by exploring the solid facets of this Christian life: our theology; the non-negotiables, if you will, of what it means to be a disciple. We will then move to the liquid implementation of it and how to live it out personally: our methodology and what it means to make disciples. Then we will conclude with the gaseous, or expansive, multiplication of faith—our missiology. Welcome to Kung Fu Theology.

Chapter 1
Discussion Questions

1. What are you hoping to get out of this book?

2. What is one area of your faith where you need to grow?

3. For you, are you experiencing more maturity in being a disciple, or in making disciples?

4. Reread 1 Corinthians 9:19-23. Who do you know who lives this out effectively? What do they do?

5. What are some of the obstacles you, or others, face in entering into other people's communities, circles, or culture?

CHAPTER 2

Believe

"That is why we labor and strive, because we have put our hope in the living God, who is the Savior of all people, and especially of those who believe." 1 Timothy 4:10

"God isn't looking for people of great faith, but for individuals ready to follow Him." Hudson Taylor

Let me tell you a story. I could've saved a lot of time. Being twenty-two and fresh out of college, I didn't have a handbook of how to do ministry. I looked at the Bible and saw principles, but I didn't see any methodology of how to reach high schoolers. I knew a couple of things though—God called me to preach the Gospel to all creation, and I was at South Kitsap High School, then the largest high school in the state of Washington. Football was huge on the Kitsap Peninsula and I thought a home game would be a great venue to reach out to the students about the launching of Young Life. Using Print Shop Deluxe, I printed nearly a thousand invitations on quarter sheets of paper which had a pixelated rocketship with, "Young Life is taking off! Come join us!" printed beneath it. That night, I passed out all 1,000 of them to students who had never met me and only heard the words, "Here, come join us." My excitement grew as the stack dwindled. This was going to be a start of a ministry that people would write about for years to come.

Three nights later, my wife and I stood ready for the hundreds of students who were sure to come. At 7:00, the six kids from our youth group were sitting there, and were still sitting there twenty minutes later watching a door that never opened. If crickets could have chirped then, followed by an echoing bullfrog, they would have. It was lonely and eerily silent, in a night that was supposed to change the atmosphere at the school. I imagine we still played a game of spoons, and everyone left that night wondering why no one came. One thousand invitations were now lining the bottom of a garbage can somewhere.

A centerpiece of Young Life ministry is the camp experience. Malibu, nestled in British Columbia, is possibly the greatest youth camp property that Young Life owns. Thousands of kids have put their faith in Christ out on the dock, in their cabins, or down by the water. The echo of Chatterbox Falls in the distance juxtaposed with the random yacht making its way through the channel, creates a unique atmosphere for kids at their first Young Life experience—and what an experience it is. The natural beauty of the mountains engulfing Princess Louisa inlet, 400 kids having bellyflop contests, and a week to walk through the story of Jesus is prime real estate for seeing kids make decisions to follow Christ. And they usually do.

Eventually, after launching a Young Life club at South Kitsap High School, which would be passed to much more capable hands at the end of the year, my wife and I moved back to Spokane to teach at Rogers High School, set in the poorest zip code in the state, and to help kick off Young Life. Fortunately, the new area director, Scott, would join us and help create bridges within the school community. I was just the English teacher who felt called to love kids and show them Jesus. As camp season rolled around, Scott found a way to get scholarships for ten kids so they could go to Malibu. But he also wanted to bring Doug along. Doug was the biggest kid of all—well, a kid hiding in a grown up's body. Doug taught history at the school and hung around a lot of Young Life club nights. He would usually be the brunt of most of the games as he was 'all in,' and the kids loved him—a big defensive end-turned teacher, who had an abundance of love and an abundance of enthusiasm. Yet, he wasn't a Christ-follower. Honestly, I was shocked. We go to camp with the intention of having solid leaders who can introduce the campers to Christ, and Scott wanted to bring a leader who wasn't even a follower. Since Scott was the boss, we went with it. Doug came.

It was Wednesday night at camp. The speaker just introduced the idea of sin and Christ's work on the cross. He then told everyone to go find fifteen minutes to be by themselves and look at the wonder of God's creation and the magnificence of His love for us. I was among the last to leave and knew right where I wanted to go—Flag Rock, as it looked over the water and would be a quiet respite for a few moments. As I drew near though, I was disappointed to see a silhouette of a man who beat me to the place. I figured the rock was big enough for two, so I went and sat on the other side. And then I realized it was Doug invading my spot. "Can we talk?" Doug said in a hushed voice. I had led kids to Christ before, but never an adult. I knew the questions would be harder, and the answers had to be better; I was only 25 and my studies were at Washington State University's English center, not a seminary. Doug really only asked one question that night: "How can I have this life the speaker is talking about?" And that was why Scott wanted Doug to come along. He knew the gospel was irresistible. And for me, it was that night theology became simple. Sanctification, atonement, propitiation, righteousness—lots of big words. I just pointed Doug to Matthew 4:19: "Follow me and I will make you a fisher of men." It was that simple. Jesus never told us to pray a prayer, check a box, or recite a scripted prayer. He said, "Follow me." And that's where Doug started—choosing to follow Christ that night. His fear was that God would ask him to do something that he didn't want to. To give up important things like his golf game, coaching, or something like that. But the second part of Matthew 4:19 brought solace to that: "I will make...." I just told Doug that the Holy Spirit will begin to transform him and his desires. But golf would more than likely be OK. The part that excited Doug the most was the third part: "Fishers of men." He would be the one who got to tell others about Jesus, and he began by telling his wife. Doug, a new man, was now a follower of Christ, becoming changed by Christ, and on mission with Christ.

The final night at Malibu is traditionally known as 'Say-So' night, where kids would declare their decisions to follow Jesus. Hands would go up, the student would stand, and tell of his or her decision. I'll never forget the look on the speaker's face when Doug raised his hand. "Do you want to say something?" he asked Doug with a quizzical look. "Yep. Last night I chose to follow Christ!" The place went crazy. I caught Scott's eye and he just gave me that knowing smile of understanding the power of the cross. Thirty-some years later, it's still my favorite camp story.

This idea of Kung Fu Theology was lived out at Malibu. To Scott, he embraced the simple idea in 1 Corinthians 9—"I became all things to all people so that I might win some." He met Doug, on Doug's terms, in a context Doug could understand, in a way Doug could receive. Often that's the obstacle. It's us—the church. In the West, we often create attractional models of church where the goal is to get people into our doors so that they can hear about Jesus, sit in our chairs, sing our songs, listen to our speaker. It's not that those things are wrong, it's just that they may not be the most effective method. So often in the church today, not just in the West but around the world, we spend extensive time looking at what others are doing and think if we duplicate it, we will get the same results. But obviously that is not the case. We have to go back to what we know to be true about God. In other words, what does it mean to be a disciple and have solid theology.

And this is what Jesus did. I love Matthew 9 because it melds the humanity of Christ with the divinity of Christ. At the end of Matthew 8, Jesus got in a boat and went to Capernaum. Maybe he went to a home to rest, maybe he wanted to have some alone time, or maybe he knew the story that was being written. But then at the start of chapter 9, some people brought to him a paralytic man knowing that Jesus might heal him. They came with the hope that he would, or maybe with the dread of knowing that this was their last resort—that if Jesus didn't intervene now, there was no hope. Honestly, I can relate to this.

Let me tell you a story. One day I found myself in Hefei, China at a registered church. Nothing out of the ordinary—just a couple of thousand Chinese people with the three white faces of my friends and I. As soon as the service was over, an usher came to me and, in English, said, "They want to see you upstairs." I turned to my friend and told him that either the PSB were waiting and we were being sent home, or something cool was about to happen. I told him, "Let's go and see who wants us." In all honesty, there was a bit of fear as we climbed the five flights of stairs as no one knew where we were and I had read too many stories about the persecution of believers in China. But we still followed the usher up to the 5th floor and walked into the pastor's office. We were greeted warmly and a translator communicated that they were happy to have us. We exchanged pleasantries and answered a few questions of where we were from since it was quite apparent that foreigners were...well...foreign. Despite our differences, it didn't take too long to find some similarities between our cultures and our churches. A few minutes later a knock came at the door and a couple in their mid-thirties, dressed in rags, came in. Their weathered faces reflected not just the difficult life they had lived, but also the anguish they were going through. In their hands they held x-rays of the bones of their two daughters, both suffering from Osteogenesis Imperfecta, or brittle bone disease. With tears in their eyes, I could tell they were begging for help. For something. Hope? Life? Just something. They were obviously at the end of their rope and they needed a miracle. The pastor turned to me and asked me to pray. I've read about faith. I thought I had faith. But now was the time to put my faith into action. Did I really believe that God could heal them? And this was the moment for me that I knew my theology needed to be solid. I had to believe that the Jesus I found in scripture was the same one I prayed to in that upper room. I found myself in Matthew 9 often realizing the people bringing in the paralytic probably had the same fears as they waited on Jesus. And Jesus entered their world. Like water. He told the man to pick up his bed and go home, and he did. For me, I prayed with the greatest faith I could muster that Sunday morning. This book would be much more captivating if I saw the bones strengthen right in front of me and each girl fully restored, but I didn't. I still don't know if the girls were healed. They may have been. I do know that I entered the world of this couple and did what Jesus asked of me. And that may be one of the cornerstones of being a disciple. In this equation in the upper room in Hefei, there were really three parts being played. The parents did their part—to follow the scripture in

James and ask the elders and leaders to pray. I did my part—to pray in faith to the God who can make the lame walk, the blind see, and the deaf hear. And God would do His part. Often this is the difficulty in living out the Christian life. I not only want to do my part, but sometimes I also want to do the other person's part, as well as God's part. But it doesn't work that way. I just need to do my part and believe God will do His.

Kung Fu Theology is about being liquid. Being liquid means that you form to the culture you are in, the lives you are engaged with, and the people you are connected to. The theology behind being liquid though is solid—it's unchanging, non-negotiable, and transformational. But how it is lived out is fluid. As we walk through this transition from solid to liquid to gas, the first step of defining our theology is to believe. I'm going to make the assumption that your theology of the inerrancy of Scripture, the deity of Christ, and the path of salvation is well-defined and grounded in scripture—basically that your understanding of the church doctrinal statement is Biblical and rooted in Christ. Instead, we are going to begin this book by looking at four key, solid components that are central to faith. To believe is the first. This isn't just "believe on the Lord Jesus Christ and you shall be saved." This is about searching deep within yourself and measuring whether you truly do believe what scripture says. Do you believe that the methods of

Jesus are as applicable today as they were 2000 years ago? Do you believe that God can still heal not just the brokenhearted, but the physically broken? Do you believe that God truly does hear and answer prayers? To grow in this area, you need to exercise your faith muscle. As Hebrews 11 says, "Now faith is confidence in what we hope for and assurance of what we do not see."[1] As you move from being an infant in the faith to a mature disciple, the development of faith has to be a cornerstone. The Old Testament is littered with people who have assurance in what they could not see: Abram went to the land that God would show him, Noah built a boat, Moses raised his staff at the sea, Rahab hung a scarlet cord, and Isaiah said yes. But what about you? How strong is your faith? Are you exercising your faith muscle? Are you ever in situations where you will be in trouble if God doesn't show up?

George Muller was one such man—a man who would be in great trouble if God didn't show up. During the 1800's in Bristol, England at the Orphanage at Ashley Downs, Muller cared for over 10,000 orphaned children and gave away over $100,000,000 in today's dollars. At the end of his life he said, "I have joyfully dedicated my whole life to the object of exemplifying how much may be accomplished by prayer and faith."[2] Though there are many around the world who have cared for as many, Muller "is best remembered for his complete trust in God's provision, never soliciting the community for financial donations nor accepting any government support."[3] The most popular story of Muller's ministry is the morning they had no food or milk for the children's breakfast. As usual, Muller and the children sat and prayed asking the Lord to provide. As soon as they prayed, a knock came at the door from a baker who told Muller that he couldn't sleep and decided to bake bread for the children. Then soon after, another knock came and a milkman told Muller that his truck broke down outside of the orphanage and he had gallons of milk to give the children.[4] Stories like this were not unique for Muller and for dozens of years he saw God provide again and again.

But don't get caught up in the stories of provision and miss the key point—Muller never asked anyone for help. There were no fundraising dinners, no bake sales, no matching campaigns. He prayed. His team prayed. They prayed knowing that if God didn't show up they would be in trouble. Is that how you do it? I don't. To be perfectly honest, I believe God has given me a gift of faith, but there is a fleshly piece that tells me to have a back-up plan just in case God doesn't meet the need in the way that I imagine. But if Muller were included in the Hebrews 11 faith hall of fame, it would probably read, "By faith, George Muller trusted God to provide for every daily need for 10,000 orphaned children."

So what would it say about you? Do you believe that God is who He says He is throughout scripture? Do you exercise your faith muscle? So often when we hear stories like this, we dismiss them thinking they are days gone by and don't happen anymore. Living in the West, we typically don't see the stories like Mueller's for a variety of reasons, but that doesn't mean they don't happen on a regular basis. For me, a story like Mueller's happened one night in Beijing.

Let me tell you a story. Subway line 10 was my favorite in Beijing as one could circle the entire town and be within walking distance or a short rickshaw ride away from all the major tourist stops and photo ops. But my stop that night at Suzhou Jie put me in the center of the business district. Even though it was well into the evening, the streets were still lined with cars of people trying to get home, packed restaurants that already had tables filled with empty bottles of Nanjing beer, and carts lining the sidewalks in a makeshift night market. I didn't have to walk far to find the apartment building I was looking for. Even though they are all similar in the daytime, at night it's even harder to identify your destination as there are no indicators of which building is which. Outside of each building, children were playing *jianzi*, kicking a shuttlecock back and forth, and the adults were playing badminton in the courtyard. The smell of peanut oil still wafted through the few trees as I entered the single metal door. Fortunately this building had an elevator since I was headed to the 17th floor. I've been in many buildings that hiking up flight after flight was the only option.

My host let me in his small two bedroom flat that had the typical look of every Chinese apartment I've been in—a kitchen with a hotplate, a small refrigerator, a few pieces of wooden furniture, and a wet bath with a squat pot toilet. The floor had the typical twenty-four inch tiles and a small air conditioner was hanging on the wall. Other than my host, a Chinese man who was a mutual friend was also there to serve as our translator for the evening. About halfway through our first cup of tea, the knock we had been waiting for finally came. I wasn't sure what to expect as the door opened, and wasn't too surprised when a frail little man hunched over at the waist walked in. After introductions, Mr. Z, our guest, took a seat on the floor across from the small sofa. Immediately all three of us offered our seats to the man who insisted sitting on the floor. It was strange to watch this elderly man position himself on the floor, but it was clear it was what he preferred.

After a cup of jasmine tea and a few pleasantries, he went on to tell us his story:

The Cultural Revolution was in full swing. No one was safe as the government was going after educators, and doctors, and especially church leaders. We moved from place to place trying to stay a step ahead of the police, knowing that one day the sermon I was preaching was going to be my last...well at least on the free side of the prison bars.

The night it happened, we were in an old abandoned hotel down by the river in Fuzhou. We all came separately so as not to attract attention and I arrived at the hotel after most of the others. I can still remember the musty smell of the hallways that were damp with the summer humidity mixed with the coal dust from the previous winters. As I came into the room, I was greeted by familiar faces and two or three new ones. There was no furniture in the room except for the small stools that lined the perimeter two or three deep. We sang in our usual hushed tones for nearly an hour. The worship that night was sweet as though God himself was preparing me for what came next. There was a firm knock on the door and silence immediately erased any remaining notes, and people stared wide-eyed at me as I stood to open the door. As I did four policemen burst in with nightsticks swinging wildly. Since I was in the line of sight, I was hit numerous times across the head and shoulders. My congregation froze as they did not want to be the next target and knew if they fought back, the guns strapped to the sides of the men would answer quickly.

The four men shouted that they wanted to know who was in charge. Three different men in the room stood and said that they were in order to keep me safe so I could continue to share the story of Christ with others. I knew that the police only wanted the leader in hopes that the others would flee and scatter out of fear. With blood dripping down the side of my head, I whispered, "I am the one you are looking for." I wasn't about to have anyone in my flock taken as I knew I was strong enough to withstand whatever the next weeks or months brought.

What I didn't know was that it wouldn't be months, it would be years. For nearly fifteen years I was chained to the floor of the prison. I could get up to use the toilet in the cell, but if I stood any other time I would be beaten. I quickly learned to comply and the floor became my home. That was years ago and I still find the floor the most comfortable place.

We all sat in awe while he spoke, feeling like we just lived out one of the great mission biographies in our generation of a man who no one would ever read about or even know his name. For the next hour we all went back and forth talking about the church in China, the spread of the Gospel, and future vision of the church. As we wound up our time, I asked Mr. Z one simple question, "How can we, as the Western church, pray for you?" There are few words in my life that I remember as vividly as how he answered. "Most of you pray that the persecution will end. Don't. Don't pray for it to end. Rather, pray that we will endure because that is what has made our church strong. In fact, we pray that the Western church will face persecution because your church is shallow and weak."

The entire ride home I sat in silence reflecting on his words. It was such an inverted way of thinking that made perfect sense in light of what Paul wrote in 2 Corinthians: "That is why, for Christ's sake, I delight in weaknesses, in insults, in hardships, in persecutions, in difficulties. For when I am weak, I am strong."[5]

Let's go back to the original premise of theology being solid and unwavering. Each of these true stories captures the first step of living out faith in a visible, real, tangible way—to believe. Mueller believed; Mr. Z believed; and I am growing in my unbelief.

Belief is not an academic practice because "even the demons believe that—and shudder."[6] It's so much deeper than that. It's about conviction. The conviction that this life you live is not your own; it's about putting God's will above your own; it's about having such a deep love affair with the creator of the universe that the things of the world are no longer appealing. It sounds unrealistic, but as the Chinese proverb says, "A journey of a thousand miles begins with a single step." We keep exercising our faith muscle so that a year from now we are not the same person who we are today. We begin to trust God with the little things so that when it comes time to trust Him with the big, we have a long list of mileposts that we can look back on and see His faithfulness. Just believe. And that is Kung Fu Theology.

Chapter 2
Discussion Questions

1. Who are a couple of people in your life right now who you need to engage with?

2. What are characteristics of people that you view as mature and how does faith set them apart from others?

3. How can you develop these characteristics into your own life?

4. What is your understanding of what it means to believe in Jesus?

5. How can that be lived out on a daily basis?

CHAPTER 3

Surrender

"Whoever wants to be my disciple must deny themselves and take up their cross daily and follow me. For whoever wants to save their life will lose it, but whoever loses their life for me will save it." Luke 9:23-24

"Conversion is a complete surrender to Jesus. It's a willingness to do what he wants you to do." Billy Sunday

I just wanted to enjoy nachos that night. I had been teaching English all day, and probably had played with my two-year-old, Hannah, before tucking her in. Thirty some years later I can vividly remember it. I was watching the old TV news program, *"20/20"* and there was an episode called, "The Dying Rooms."[1] It was an undercover story that the BBC aired about an orphanage in Shanghai. I had heard stories like this of babies being left to die, but nothing this real or this vivid. It was during this story that the Lord spoke to me. When I think of the Lord speaking to people, I always go back to stories like Samuel and Moses, not to some guy sitting in his recliner in the living room. I can think of a handful of times that God has spoken clearly to me in my life and this was one of them. I know it wasn't audible to others, but it was audible to my heart. "This is what I want you to be about." Nine simple words, but words that changed the destiny of a little girl, and changed the course of my life.

My wife, Carrie, and I always thought having kids would be easy and never imagined we would go through several years of infertility. We both came from families where our moms were married at 18 and had their first child nine months later. We just assumed our story would be the same. But that wasn't the case. Month after month of tears and disappointment led to year after year, until fortunately we had a little girl. It was during those years though the first conversations of adoption crossed our lips, however we became mute to it once Hannah was born. But these words I heard in my living room spoke loudly to me and reignited the conversations. I had heard of people who said God spoke to them, but never understood it until it happened to me. Somewhere deep down, I knew the Spirit was revealing himself to me and was speaking in a way that I could clearly understand. I didn't really think it through, but I said yes that night. I wasn't sure what

I was saying yes to, but I knew it was the only answer. I began thinking of my two experiences with Chinese people—walking through San Francisco's Chinatown as a ten-year-old thinking the smells were weird, and getting sick as a seventeen-year-old at my first visit to a Chinese restaurant. Now I was saying yes to adopting a Chinese child. And I said yes…and my wife said no. I understand her thinking because she had a beautiful baby girl and was now hopeful of having a second child. Plus I was the one who had seen the video and there was little chance of her ever seeing it in those days before YouTube. It wasn't the Sinai wilderness, but it felt like it.

For four years I carried the burden to adopt—even through the birth of our son two years later. I felt the Lord keep pursuing me on this. Sermons seemed to speak to it, Scripture always seemed to connect to it. I knew this was big and God would need to speak to Carrie also. So I just kept praying. At the start of December in year five of believing God was calling us to adopt, I finally reached my limit. In my journal I wrote, "God, I believe you called us to adopt from China, but I need you to speak to Carrie also. If you don't speak to her by the end of the year, I will walk away from it." As I look back now, I know that it reveals immaturity of my faith, but it is also where I was—wanting God to speak the same way to my wife as He did to me. Here's the crazy part, that night our local news channel, KXLY, ran a story on a local doctor, Dr. Stone, who just returned with a little girl from China. That was it. One story. I chronicled it in my journal the next morning wondering if this was a sign, but then there was silence for the rest of the month. In January I started putting the idea of adoption behind me even though in that deep secret place I was still holding on to it. The silence was deafening as the routines of the day continued to be drowned out by a longing in my heart to respond to what I still believed God was calling us to. And then February came. It was then that I received a call from John, a former student of mine who was attending Gonzaga University.

"Mr. Allen, this is John, from your English class last year. I know you are a big college basketball fan and you told me that you would write a letter of recommendation for me to get into Gonzaga, but if I got in, I would have to get you tickets."

I love that John remembered that because Zag tickets are impossible to come by in Spokane.

"Well, I got into Gonzaga," John continued, "and I got two tickets for you for the game in two weeks on senior night."

I was floored that he would remember that and pretty darned excited too. I immediately walked down the hallway to my best friend's classroom. Dick was as big of a fan as I was, and two weeks later we were walking into the Martin Center to watch Gonzaga play Pepperdine. A line of students about 1,500 deep, who had slept outside all week to get good seats, were standing at one door waiting to get in. The usher who helped us said we had special media passes and to stand at the adjacent door which was about ten feet away from the students and had no one in line. Obviously, we weren't too popular with the kids as sleeping outside in the cold Spokane night caused a bit of resentment towards two guys who got to bypass the suffering. In the fifteen minutes we waited for the doors to open, only one other couple came to our line. As the four of us talked, it wasn't too long before the wife asked where we were sitting. "On the students' side," I replied. "What about you?"

"We're on the reserved side about center court and two-thirds of the way up. Do you want to switch tickets?"

I've been a sports fan for a long time but I have never been asked to switch tickets. After hearing their explanation of how they like sitting on the student side so they can scream, and dance, and jump around, we said yes. Center court sounded great. So we switched tickets, the doors opened, they went to the left, and we went to the right. The seats were exactly as described—perfect seats for what would be a fantastic game. We hadn't been in the seats much more than a minute when a man came and sat in the seat directly behind me. I leaned over to Dick and whispered, "I know this guy. Not sure how, but I know him." As the last words left my lips, a woman came down the aisle holding a one-year-old Chinese baby. "You're Dr. Stone!" I said as I whirled around while his wife was getting settled. "Weren't you on the news a couple of months ago?" During the next 30 minutes waiting for the game to start, I heard about their story, exchanged numbers, and got in contact with their social worker who would talk to my wife the next day. All because of tickets I shouldn't have gotten, in a seat where I shouldn't have been, next to a guy I had never met. And that's how God chose, five years later, to put in motion His words He spoke to me in my living room: "This is what I want you to be about."

The next week we were invited by the social worker to a citizenship ceremony for about a dozen Chinese kids who were all newly adopted. There was a sense of wonder as we arrived not knowing exactly what we were walking into. We sat in the back and the tears came quickly to me...and to Carrie. Each family was introduced and our U.S. Representative presented their child as citizens. We walked out that day, sat in our car, and looked at each other. She said one word, "Yes." We were going to start the process of adopting a Chinese baby. There weren't fireworks, or trumpets, but there was a sense of awe and joy unlike anything before. It really did feel like the day when Carrie told me she was pregnant after four years of trying, something far beyond the human realm.

Obedience can feel arbitrary. It can feel optional. It can feel subjective. But as scripture is opened, it seems to be the foundational principle that separates those who experience a depth of intimate relationship with the Lord from those who long for it. So often I see people trying to attach Biblical obedience with behavior modification similar to a child not touching the stove or a dog not jumping on the sofa. But it is so much deeper. Back in Jeremiah, God says, "Obey my voice, and I will be your God, and you will be my people; and you will walk in all the ways which I have commanded you, that it may be well with you."[2] But this obedience that God is asking for is not a behavioral response. It is rooted in surrendering—surrendering your will and ultimately your life.

This surrender is the second foundational idea behind the solid part of faith of Kung Fu Theology— first we believe, and then we surrender. For my wife and I, obedience, rooted in surrendering, kept growing as God called us to adopt a second, and then a third child. Then to leave good jobs. To sell good houses. To take cuts in pay. But surrender is not just found in the big decisions. Often, those can be easier than the daily surrender of the little things, as it's the little things that are often rooted in comfortable living. Karl Barth referred to comfort as one of the great sirens of the age.[3] And it's true. Back in my English teacher days, I taught The Odyssey multiple times. I would have kids act out their favorite scene and every semester the two most popular were Polyphemus the Cyclops, and the story of the Sirens. The Siren group would put their Odysseus in the center of the room and tie him up to a chair and put ear plugs in his ears. Then the "Sirens" would sit in all four corners of the room and try to lure Odysseus their direction. They would do all sorts of crazy things—in one corner the Siren would seductively hold Twinkies and Coke; in another the Siren would hold trophies and medals; in the third, the Siren would hold up posters of famous actresses or singers; and in yet another, the Siren would hold up money. Each would do their best to get Odysseus to lean their way. And with faith, it often isn't much different. And the Siren that lures us away the most from the things of God and the words of Scripture is comfort.

I want to be careful as I write these chapters because there is a tendency for pastors and leaders to use their life experiences to be the primary motivator for people, as opposed to pointing people back to Scripture. At the end of the day, my hope is not that readers will treat my life stories as normative, but that they will serve as an inspiration of how one may have his life intersect with God, and how God desires to write a similar story in each of you. I love how Mother Teresa depicts this idea: "I am a little pencil in the hand of a writing God, who is sending a love letter to the world."[4] It's in the pages of this love story that God moves you, as the main character, through trials and victories, introduces new people to the story, and takes you down winding paths unfolding the story in front of you as you anticipate what the next chapter holds.

It's on these winding paths that we can look at a few Biblical characters who have the same response when encountering God. Abraham, as he reached out his hand to slay his son, heard God call out to him, "Abraham! Abraham!" And Abraham uttered three words, "Here I am."[5] Moses had God call out to him from the burning bush, "Moses! Moses!" And Moses uttered three words, "Here I am."[6] Samuel, who thinking it was Eli, had God call out to him, "Samuel, Samuel!" And Samuel uttered three words, "Here I am."[7] And finally, Isaiah heard the voice of the Lord asking whom He should send. And Isaiah uttered three words, "Here I am."[8] Four mighty men of scripture all uttered the same phrase, which is translated from one simple Hebrew word—Hineni. I would guess for most of you, you are unfamiliar with this word, but when we talk about surrender, this may be the image that captures it best. In saying, "Here I am," these men did not reply saying they are physically present, but hineni is loosely translated as, "Whatever you are about to ask, I am already in agreement with it."[9] Think carefully for a moment about what hineni means and what Abraham, Moses, Samuel, and Isaiah are saying. No matter what the Lord is about to ask them at that point, they are going to say yes. I know for me, when I talk to people about what surrender looks like, it can become such an abstract concept, but a tangible way to encourage and grow in surrendering is by saying hineni. For most people, myself included, it's the first part of the phrase where the obstacle lies—'whatever you you are about to ask.' We know God is loving and kind and gracious, but what if He asks us to do something far beyond what we think we are capable, or worse yet, something we just don't want to do. It seems comical, but I think about when Moses finally said, "Send someone else."[10] Isn't that the cry of so many of us, for God to ask the hard things of someone else? But, as our faith grows, we should be surrendering more and more so that we can honestly say, "Whatever you are about to ask, I am already in agreement with it." I'm already in agreement, not that I will eventually agree. But right now. Today. How it is played out may be revealed in the coming months or even years, but to be in a place of surrender is saying, "Not my will, but your will be done in my life."

A demonstration of saying yes might be best given through missionary Adoniram Judson and his wife Ann. When Adoniram was courting her back in the 1800's, he penned a letter to her father saying:

> *I have now to ask whether you can consent to part with your daughter early next spring, to see her no more in this world? Whether you can consent to her departure to a heathen land, and her subjection to the hardships and sufferings of a missionary life? Whether you can consent to her exposure to the dangers of the ocean; to the fatal influence of the southern climate of India; to every kind of want and distress; to degradation, insult, persecution, and perhaps a violent death? Can you consent to all this, for the sake of Him who left His heavenly home and died for her and for you; for the sake of perishing, immortal souls; for the sake of Zion and the glory of God? Can you consent to all this, in hope of soon meeting your daughter in the world of glory, with a crown of righteousness brightened by the acclamations of praise which shall redound to her Savior from heathens saved, through her means, from eternal woe and despair?[11]*

Imagine as a father of a young daughter what you would do if you received this letter. A crazy young man wants to go to a far away land and take your daughter knowing that they both may die and you will, more than likely, never see her again. And this young man wants you to say yes. I don't know about you, but I have four daughters and as of this writing, I've had two conversations with young men wanting to marry the eldest two. Jason and Johnny are incredible young men, growing in faith, and love my girls dearly. But our conversation centered more around their commitment to loving them, providing for them, putting their needs above their own—all noble and what I would hope to hear, but it wasn't Judson's words of taking them away to serve the Lord and most likely die.

But the story of Judson continues. He then writes to his prospective wife, Ann:

> *If our lives are preserved and our attempt prospered, we shall next new year's day be in India, and perhaps wish each other a happy new year in the uncouth dialect of Hindostan or Burmah. We shall no more see our kind friends around us, or enjoy the conveniences of civilized life, or go to the house of God with those that keep holy day; but swarthy countenances will everywhere meet our*

eye, the jargon of an unknown tongue will assail our ears, and we shall witness the assembling of the heathen to celebrate the worship of idol gods. We shall be weary of the world, and wish for wings like a dove, that we may fly away and be at rest. We shall probably experience seasons when we shall be exceeding sorrowful, even unto death. We shall see many dreary, disconsolate hours, and feel a sinking of spirits, anguish of mind, of which now we can form little conception. O, we shall wish to lie down and die. And that time may soon come. One of us may be unable to sustain the heat of the climate and the change of habits; and the other may say, with literal truth, over the grave—'By foreign hands thy dying eyes were closed; By foreign hands thy decent limbs composed; By foreign hands thy humble grave adorned;' but whether we shall be honored and mourned by strangers, God only knows. At least, either of us will be certain of one mourner. In view of such scenes shall we not pray with earnestness 'O for an overcoming faith,'?[12]

I am greatly convicted by the words of Judson, his wife's agreement to say yes, and her father's agreement. This isn't the message that's preached in

most churches or in most living room small groups.
But it seems scriptures like Galatians 2:20, "I have
been crucified with Christ and I no longer live, but
Christ lives in me. The life I now live in the body I
live by faith in the Son of God who loved me and gave
himself for me," are not taken as they were intended.
I have had the privilege to travel all over the world
and the message in most places is different than it
is in the West. There's a cost to following Jesus that
we don't see or hear here. A few years ago, I was
sitting in the Philippines with pastors from the U.S.,
Uganda, Ethiopia, China, and the Philippines. The
Chinese pastors led us in a song that morning with the
words, "My blood will pour out in the sand and I will
glorify the Lord." They were all weeping as they sang
due to their burden for the unengaged in the Middle
East, and I'm staring in disbelief at my American
friends knowing we sing songs like, "Stand in your
Love," "Good, Good Father," and "Counting Every
Blessing." This chapter is not a critique of Western
worship, but revealing the mindset that we often avoid.
There is a cost to following Jesus. As we surrender
more and more, it costs us more and more. And it's not
just lyrics to a song. My Chinese friends are willing to
lay their lives down if it means people in the Middle
East experience eternal life and see a disciple-making
movement begin.

As we go back to Scripture, Luke writes in his gospel:

> Large crowds were traveling with Jesus, and turning to them he said: 'If anyone comes to me and does not hate father and mother, wife and children, brothers and sisters—yes, even their own life—such a person cannot be my disciple. And whoever does not carry their cross and follow me cannot be my disciple."[13]

And that's what surrendering is all about—giving up everything—dying to yourself and following Christ, no matter the cost.

At my position at the church, my friends on staff always give me a hard time because most of my pop culture references are from the 80's. I'd rather use a reference from Ferris Bueller or Huey Lewis than Marvel or Beyonce. I try to convince them that there are greater redemptive analogies and literary merit to the things of the past, but it's hard to convince someone of the merit of Rocky sequels and big hair bands as sermon illustrations. But there is one that I hold fast to. Steve Camp was one of my favorite Christian singers in the 80's and I still have one of his songs at the top of my Spotify list. The lyrics of, "Whatever You Ask," capture this idea of surrendering: "Lord, whatever You ask I want to obey You, To let my life beat with a servant's heart, Lord whatever You ask I know that You can give me wisdom and courage to equal the task, whatever You ask."[14] I hear the word 'hineni' throughout this song. And I reflect daily on whether I can honestly say, "Whatever you are about to ask, I'm already in agreement with it."

In January 2013, I found myself on a ferry from Hong Kong to Cheung Chau island. The previous day I had dropped off my oldest daughter, Grace, at the YWAM base in the area and I had a day to myself prior to flying home. For the past six months, my wife and I had been praying about planting a church in our area in Eastern Washington. We had committed families, we had some experience, and we had a vision for what it might look like. We just didn't have a clear answer from the Lord. At least not yet.

The thirty-five minute ferry ride isn't too long, and the views are spectacular. Seeing the International Commerce Center skyscraper as a sentinel at the entrance to the harbor on one side, and Victoria Peak on the other, honestly may be the most magnificent view one can find in Asia. That day I was sitting on the top deck just talking with the Lord about what was next and what He may have for us. When I asked Him the question about whether we were to plant a church, the answer was clear and concise, "No." I can think of a handful of times where I specifically heard something clearly from the Lord, and this one was unmistakable.

I've shared this story numerous times and people tend to want to know the same thing. Was it audible? Did anyone else hear it? How did you know? Here's what I do know. God has spoken to people for centuries, and the sheep know the shepherd's voice. As J.D. Greear says, "The spirit inside you, is better than Jesus beside you."[15] I know no one else heard it, but it was audible to me. We had been seeking an answer and in a remote part of the world, He finally spoke. The hard part was that it was not the answer I was expecting, or honestly, wanting. For the remaining fifteen minutes of the ferry ride I remember asking the Lord over and over, "Are you sure? Are you sure?" It seems comical now that I would sit and question the Lord's wisdom, and I now wonder if I was asking that question of the Lord, or asking myself if I heard correctly. The next day I flew home and shared with my wife, Carrie, what the Lord was speaking to me. In hindsight, I now see the Lord's wisdom in this as He continues to position me in a place of mobilization and multiplication in what is a much better fit for my giftings and passions. But surrendering to this was still hard. It's a bit...ok...it's a lot easier to surrender to the Lord in areas that are already in alignment with your sense of direction. The question becomes, is there a same willingness when He asks you to surrender to something that is a stretch... uncomfortable...or even painful.

With Kung Fu Theology, the willingness for a Christ follower to form into the culture is critical, but it can't be at the expense of the solid, non-negotiables of faith. Surrendering is a core principle of the solid parts of this faith journey we are on and it keeps us on a Christ-led trajectory. It's impossible to create a formulaic, linear path for spiritual growth, but there are principles that seem to develop sequentially. First you believe, then you surrender, and then you begin to experience the power that God promises. It's with that power that we find ourselves being transformed more and more. And that's how Kung Fu Theology develops.

Chapter 3
Discussion Questions

1. Have you ever said *'Hineni'* to the Lord? Whatever He was about to ask of you, you were already in agreement with it?

2. How is your struggle with comfort? Is comfort winning at this stage in your life?

3. What area of your life do you find that you need to surrender?

4. Practically, what does that surrender look like?

5. The author talks about hearing God speak to him. Have you ever heard the Lord speak to you? What was the situation and what did He say? How did it change you?

CHAPTER 4

Power

"Your faith might not rest on human wisdom, but on God's power." 1 Cor. 2:5

"God uses men who are weak and feeble enough to lean on Him." Hudson Taylor

Cairo, for me, was not Indiana Jones, nor was it Lara Croft. It was a juxtaposition between the modern and the past, the desert and the river. In one moment I was at Pizza Hut staring across the street at the Giza pyramids encased by sand and history, the next I was on the pyramid staring at a city skyline that Ramses himself could not have imagined. The contrast of the two was seen across the city—massive highways winding around ancient mausoleums, and fashionable businessmen briskly walking past tunic-wearing street vendors. But this was the contrast I longed to witness. In Washington State, it's pretty homogenous economically, socially, and racially. It's this contrast that Paul identifies when he says, "to the Jew I became a Jew, and to the Gentile, I became a Gentile."[1] Possibly the greatest struggle for cross-cultural workers today is that assimilation into another culture—when in China, to become Chinese, and in Egypt to become Egyptian.

My fourth night in Cairo I was introduced to a pastor of a Sudanese refugee church. I honestly don't think there was another man on the planet from a more different culture than I was—he lived in a tribe, in a war-torn land, watched his family slaughtered, had no food, and was displaced to a metropolis where he didn't know the language or the culture. Yet it didn't take long for the two of us to quickly become friends and, a few hours later, I found myself preaching at his midweek service along with my Chinese friends who were with me. As is customary, we all sat on stage while about 200 people poured into a small, sweltering Catholic chapel anticipating something that I thought I knew but quickly realized that I had drifted from. I've been in a few African worship services in Uganda, but this was different. In 2020, when I woke up in the ICU after open heart surgery, I only wanted one thing—a sip of water. Anything to quench the thirst that had built up over hours and hours of surgery. Words can't accurately describe the soothing sensation that one small sip provided. That's what it felt like in that room—200 refugees wanting a sip of water, the life-giving water that only Jesus can provide. And this water provided power. What they lacked in possessions, they made up for in power. As the worship started, I could almost tangibly sense the physical presence of the Holy Spirit.

Now, before I move on, some of you are probably thinking that I got caught up in the emotional dancing and singing, and since it was such a contrast to my Western training, I mistook excitement and jubilee for the person of the Holy Spirit. Is that what you thought? Over the years I've been in every conceivable situation— praying silently in a Chinese house church, shouting praises in the aisles of the Philippines, highfiving people in the rows of Costa Rica, and everything from ultraconservative to charismatic across the Northwest. That wasn't what happened that night.

Eliana was my translator as I preached about Exodus 4 when God asks Moses what was in his hand. As a speaker it's easy to read the engagement level of your audience. Teaching *Julius Caesar* to fifteen-yearold boys over the years…not too much engagement. Telling 200 Sudanese that God has equipped them to reach the nations…quite a bit. After an hour of preaching and another hour of worshipping, the pastor asked my Chinese friend and I if we would pray for people who came forward. And come they did. I stood with Eliana on my left, and Pastor F from China stood three feet to my right with his translator.

Coming toward me was a woman in her forties with a boy who seemed about ten, while an elderly gentleman walked up to Pastor F. By this time we were all dripping in sweat, as the humidity and the human aroma hung in the room. As I looked at the boy, I noticed his hands were all shriveled up. The woman didn't need to speak as the eyes of a mother spoke volumes wanting her son to be whole again. By the time I started praying, the drumming had begun and people were filling the room with praises, oblivious to the young boy in front of me. I laid my hands on him and prayed boldly as Eliana translated everything. I believe that God still makes the lame walk, the blind see, the deaf hear, and the dead breathe. And I prayed with that confidence. And I prayed. And I prayed. As I opened my eyes, and moved my hands, his hands were still shriveled. Unchanged.

But, as I looked at Eliana, tears were now streaming down her face. All I could muster in my disappointment was, "What's wrong?"

"Your friend. The Chinese man..." she said. I had heard Pastor F praying boldly over the older man in front of him, but had no idea what Eliana was talking about. "Your friend. He prayed for my grandfather. He was deaf, and now he can hear!" I turned my head and three feet from me were two men who lived thousands of miles apart embracing each other as the man was healed. I wanted to tell the woman in front of me to go to that line because apparently that was where the power was that night. Why one got healed and not the other, I have no deep theological answer for you. But I know God's ways are much higher than mine and I trust what He did that night.

Years later, I still don't fully know what to do with that scene. But I know it was the power of God. I have no doubt and it was just three feet from me. I think that's the power Acts 1:8 speaks of, "You will receive power when the Holy Spirit comes on you." And that is the third non-negotiable solid principle of Kung Fu Theology. First you believe, then you surrender, and then you discover the power available to you. For without that power, you will not walk in the fullness of what God has designed for you. You will not live in the freedom and deliverance He has for you. And you will not discover the riches of the gospel which is "the power of God unto salvation."[2]

This chapter isn't a treatise on the manifestation of God's power after the resurrection of Jesus. But what I want to do is challenge you to not just believe, but to surrender and come to the end of yourself so that you can be filled with the Spirit of God and walk in the authority and victory that is available to you, and to impact the culture around you not by your own merit, but on the magnificence of God.

This idea of power in Scripture is something that I sometimes think we make too unreachable, and sometimes too foreign. The fact these were the last words that Jesus spoke before ascending to heaven have to carry a certain importance and priority. The final words, the last sentence, the final charge to his followers before he left them, and he chose this: "You will receive power when the Holy Spirit comes upon you."[3] Paul was a personal witness to the power when he was struck blind as he encountered the Lord on the road to Damascus. He wrote about it in several of his letters to the church. To the church at Ephesus, he wrote, "I also pray that you will understand the incredible greatness of God's power for us who believe him."[4] It's that understanding that I think we lack in the West. So much of our discipleship process is rooted in tasks and development as though it is an academic course—read this, listen to this, memorize this. But the core of life transformation is not in the checklist; it's in the everyday encounter with a living God who lives in us and provides the power to overcome sin. He helps us find freedom from our hurts, habits, and hang ups; He calms the storm that rages inside of us; He convicts us of wrongdoing; He heals the physical wounds that we can see and the emotional ones we can't; He reconciles the broken relationships in our life; and He sanctifies us as we become more like Christ. Paul knew we can't do this on our own, but so often we live like we can. And that's how this idea of power connects with the previous idea of surrender. Each day means surrendering once again and, as Paul told the Ephesians, "God, who is able, through his mighty power at work within us, to accomplish infinitely more than we might ask or think."[5]

How that power manifests is often a mystery. I sometimes long to see the miraculous, the tangible evidence of the invisible God. But often I overlook the daily evidence of the fruit of the Spirit who lives in us. As Paul wrote, "The fruit of the Spirit is love, joy, peace, patience, kindness, goodness, faithfulness, gentleness and self-control."[6] I can't discredit this fruit as being less significant than the Sudanese man getting his hearing back, for both are evidence of the power of God.

But this idea of Kung Fu Theology is rooted in walking in God's power. You will never experience the fullness of a life with Christ, nor the life of being liquid in a culture that is fast becoming more and more polarizing without being filled daily with the Spirit. Start the day by surrendering to Him and committing to follow Him even if you feel ill-equipped or weak. Scripture says, "My grace is sufficient for you, for power is perfected in weakness. Most gladly, therefore, I will rather boast about my weaknesses, so that the power of Christ may dwell in me."[7] There is no magic prayer or formula; it's just one person on their knees asking for more of Jesus and less of themselves. And that's how you start walking in power. In today's culture there is a tendency to chase the sensational, to idolize the dramatic, but the power of God often shows itself like it did to Elijah in a gentle whisper.[8] I find it's the whispers that are frequent and unless I am in a position of being still before the Lord, I often don't hear them, and very often don't obey them.

Let me tell you a story. The summer mornings in Langfang are quite pleasant compared to the smoggy sky of Beijing just an hour or two up the road. That particular morning was what I had always imagined rural China being. As I exited the orphanage compound, the cicadas were still chirping, and the nannies were just hanging their first load of laundry on the nearby lines. The humidity from the previous day still hung in the air but without the oppressiveness that the afternoons held. Summer wasn't pleasant in that area of China, as it was similar to Guangzhou and Hong Kong in the south, where activities ceased midday and meals were eaten late. Though it was still early, the babies were waking up and a few of the older kids were already moving about. The location of this center is quite unique as just a block away was a village that seemed to have never moved beyond the 1800s. The dirt roads wound through the hutongs seemingly without a lot of planning. Early morning in the neighborhoods are my favorite in China as the still of the night is present but little vignettes are dotted all around. As the four of us walked, to our right was an elderly man sitting on a three-legged stool smoking his long, curved pipe. He stared off into the nearby garden, and even as we approached, his eyes never moved. He fixated on the vegetables as though willing them to grow. What I didn't notice at the time was the four-foot high mound of dirt in the corner of the field that was one of his ancestor's burial mounds. Surely this was a reminder that his son would one day sit on that same stool and watch over his garden...and his father.

A few doors down an elderly woman was picking the last of the persimmons on the tree and offered one to each of us. I knew she said *"Zaoshang hao"* or "Good morning", but beyond that, I couldn't make out anything else. We said our customary *"Xie xie"* thanking her for the gifts, and like all Chinese people who I speak to, she giggled at our attempt to speak their language.

Around the corner was what I was looking for, and they were already working. Fry bread is my favorite morning treat in China. It's not that it's particularly good, it's just a unique experience watching the process. The same elderly couple that I would see in future years and trips were standing in front of a weathered wooden table with a piece of metal on the top, a vat of some type of cooking oil, and a mound of dough. And this is where my Mandarin language studies would always fail me. I wanted to say, "We would like 12 pieces of bread please," but it ended up with my friend and I holding up 12 fingers, pointing at the dough, and then simulating them giving it to us. Apparently, since they only sold one thing, our pantomiming was sufficient as they started at the dough. I have no idea what was in it since there were no ingredients around, just a table, some dough and a quickly growing crowd of villagers coming to watch the foreigners eat breakfast. Grandparents near us would push their grandsons to us encouraging them to speak. "Hello!" came frequently from every child and a few of the grandfathers. Our reply of "Hi" was met with laughter, the people talking to each other in Chinese, and then laughing some more. My three friends were similar to me—all over six foot, wearing shorts and a t-shirt, and significantly heavier than any of those in the crowd. The woman making the fried bread was my favorite though. While she pulled the dough into long strips, she would speak to all of her neighbors, point to us, and then they would all laugh. It was comical because the four of us still had no idea of what was being said, but it felt endearing. Or, at some level, mocking. The twelve strips of dough would be placed in the oil, and it was like a donut-making factory began. Except it was gritty, black oil and they were turned with the same chopsticks that had just fallen on the ground, and there wasn't icing or sugar anywhere to be found. The bread looked like a maple bar of sorts, and puffed up into a relatively flaky piece of bread. She took them out one by one with the same chopsticks, put them in a plastic bag, and handed them to us. Ordering wasn't the only difficult part of this journey, paying for things was always an adventure too. I wasn't too sure what she said, but it sounded like *"Wo kuai"* or five dollars. It amounted to about 90 cents, which seemed fair, and everyone was pretty delighted by these foreigners who walked into their village.

It wasn't a long walk back to the orphanage and the bread was a truly cultural experience that would make for easy conversation for the four of us on our return. Walking down the road we had farmland on one side, with corn about ready to harvest, and small brick homes on the other. As we approached where the man with the pipe had been sitting, he was now squatting on the ground tilling his soil. His plot near the house was about 20 feet by 40 feet. I would have expected him to have a hoe or shovel, but in his right hand was a piece of wire about the size and thickness of a pencil. He would stick it in the ground, lift up the dirt, and then move about an inch to his right and repeat the same steps.

This man wore the same Mao suit as did so many older men in the area. His balding head was obviously weathered from what was probably years of farming. Though the ground around him was just as weathered, there was a tenderness in each probe into the soil.

As the four of us walked by eating our fry bread, he glanced up from his work and met my eyes. We held the gaze for several seconds, as two men whose worlds intersected for a moment, trying to find one piece of common ground. He still had hours of work to do, so he put his head down and dug one more time. I turned my head and took another bite of bread. As I walked back through the gate of the orphanage, I stopped in my tracks as the Holy Spirit whispered to me, "Why didn't you stop and help that man?" Jesus spent his whole life stopping for people—Zacchaeus in the tree, Bartimaeus on the road, the Samaritan woman at the well, and yet I walked right on by. I was on a mission trip and I walked past a person who needed help. And that conviction, at that moment, was more impactful than if the Lord had turned our 12 pieces of bread into a hundred and we fed the entire village. The Spirit of conviction is founded in power. The fact that the Holy Spirit would choose to indwell a sinful man like myself and choose to speak to him, stuns me. It convinced me that the power of God is present every day, and if I would just choose to surrender to him, my life would be transformed and so would the lives of those around me.

This process of Kung Fu Theology really *is* simple... until it's not. It's not hard because God makes it hard, it's hard because I keep walking in the flesh and letting my own will supersede His. Often, even in my position of daily surrender, I still try to do things in my own power. It's when I make that shift that I experience God's power in me that can accomplish infinitely more than I may ask or think. And that's why power is a solid aspect of faith—it's essential to living the Spirit-filled life, and it's essential to Kung Fu Theology.

Chapter 4
Discussion Questions

1. How have you seen God's power evident in your own life?

2. Who do you know who seems to be walking in the power that Paul refers to in Ephesians 3:20?

3. Of the fruits of the Spirit listed in Galatians 5:22, which of the nine are you experiencing a growing maturity, and which do you need to develop?

4. Much of the time, we think of God's power being shown in the miraculous and supernatural. How else do you see God's power evident?

5. What are two or three daily practices you can implement to begin relying on God's power more than your own skills and talents?

CHAPTER 5

Brokenness

"What does the Lord require of you? To act justly and to love mercy and to walk humbly with your God." Micah 6:8

"God cannot fix whoever is first not broken." Jack Wellman

Believe. Surrender. Power. These three concepts seem foreign to today's Western Christian. The typical message to a seeker of the Gospel is rarely laced with these ideas, but they are solid core theological principles that are the bedrock of an unshakeable faith. But there is one more idea that, in my experience, is the difference of those with contagious, infectious faith, and those who often don't seem to have experienced life transformation—brokenness.

Let me tell you a story. Fortunately, the wind wasn't blowing that day because we drove through miles and miles of sandy landscape. It shouldn't have been surprising because the Middle East was just that—sandy. Barren. Desolate. I could imagine Moses leading the Israelites through this land, and from what I saw through the window of my air-conditioned van, I might have revolted too after a few hours wandering in this desert. Trips like this are always an adventure when I'm with trusted people and literally have no idea where I am going or what is going to happen once I arrive. And today was no different. The life outside the window was actually no different than that of the Chinese farmer, the Filipino worker, or the combine driver on the Palouse. Each was working hard to provide for his family, and today was the same as yesterday, and also tomorrow. The shepherd out the driver-side window was the one who caught my eye though. With several dozen sheep grazing in a drying meadow, he sat under the one shade tree on the land with three lambs hidden around his feet. His once white tunic was now stained with months of work rescuing sheep in the ditch, or correcting the wayward lamb. And his face was no different. The deep creases emulated the parched land around him, both longing for a sip of water.

As the van rolled into the village, it could have been any of the hundreds of small villages we had driven by that week. There were no identifying landmarks, and each building was made by the same stone or mud as the thousands of others I had seen. But this village seemed a bit more of a community than most. People were all sitting together talking amongst themselves, and like every other time I stepped out of a van in a distant land with a few other foreigners, the volume and giggles began to grow in intensity. The first few times in my journey, this was always uncomfortable and awkward until I realized that a foreigner was such an uncommon sight that it may actually feel like the circus had come to town. Over the years strangers have touched my daughter's blonde hair, rubbed my stomach, commented on a friend's weight, and taken photo after photo of the oddities we were. I would always try to tell my first-timers who traveled with me what was awaiting them, but I finally gave up and thought it best for them to experience those moments just like I did on that very first international trip stepping off the plane in Beijing. I would guess we probably found the head coverings and burkas as unique as they found my Mariners' cap.

We followed our leader up the four flights of stairs to a room about the size of a school classroom filled with seventy-five traditionally dressed women. I soon found out that many were born-again Christians, but most were raised much differently as one would expect in an unengaged area of the world. In moments like these, it always tends to be a sensory overload. The two fans in the corner did little to lower the temperature, and the smell of tea and fresh biscuits countered that, which usually accompanies a cramped room of hard-working people in poor communities. To the American nose, it was strong, but I would guess that none of the locals thought twice about it. The worship that morning was so pure and sweet. One man with a guitar would sing a short phrase and the women would sing it back. I've seen it done that way in VBS summer camps in the states and even in a few church services, but this one was different. Women were weeping as they sang, with their faces anguished from what was probably decades of oppression and mistreatment. Listening, I was reminded of Revelation 7 where people from every tribe, tongue, and nation were gathered around the throne singing His praises. This was so genuine and so heartfelt that I could have returned home that day knowing I had just encountered the living God.

On days like these there is not a lot of planning or preparation. I always tell people to have a sermon in their pocket and be ready to speak at any moment. The day before, we were in a larger room with kids and women singing songs and watching skits, and our host whispered in my ear a message that I relayed to my son-in-law. "Jason, they would like you to speak about love and marriage." Jason is a great speaker, but my response to his question of "When?" startled him a bit—"In about four minutes after this song is over." Today though it was my turn and fortunately I had about twenty minutes to gather my thoughts to speak to a roomful of Middle Eastern women, most of whom had Muslim backgrounds. I always begin by praying, and as I did, outside the open window behind me the Muslim call to prayer, the *Dhuhr*, echoed through the alleyways creating a tangible dichotomy that everyone in the room felt. It's easy to pray for Muslims while I was sitting in my living room in Washington, but that moment in an obscure village ruined me. It felt like a million Muslims were in the room shouting the same words that I would imagine the prophets of Baal shouted back at Elijah as he taunted them during Baal's silence.

As profound as that was, it was the ministry time after that revealed to me the deeper realities of this clash of worlds. We each had a translator and a few people in line to receive prayer. The first in my line was the mom wanting prayer that her son would follow Jesus; the second was the same but for her husband. But it was the last two who broke my heart. Woman three shared the story of her abortion that she was forced to have by her husband. This woman just wept right in front of me the tears that only a mother can have over losing a child. And the fourth woman was much more hushed. Her voice quivered as she whispered to me that she was cheating on her husband and had no one to tell. I pointed out the local leaders, and a few women who seemed so genuine in their worship. In hushed tones she just said that she can't tell anyone because, if found out, she would be killed. Not divorced, or sent away...killed. The guilt of her sin was so heavy and she so wanted to repent and be made clean. Then she fell in my arms crying on my shoulder. Her tears came from a place deep within one whose paths I don't know if I have ever walked. A place where she had no option but God.

And that's where brokenness begins—coming to the end of yourself, to a place of utter dependence on a God who is the only one who can help and heal. And so many people never get to that place of brokenness, where they depend more upon God than upon themselves. These other solid parts of theology: believe, surrender, and power will never be fully experienced until there is a deep brokenness where the reality of sin and separation is salved by the grace and love of the Savior. But here's the difficult thing, brokenness can't necessarily be taught, it has to be experienced. It really starts when one feels the magnitude of their sin and the separation from the Father. It was felt by the Samaritan woman; it was felt by Peter after his catch of fish saying he is a sinful man; it was felt by Zacchaeus as the Lord dined at his house; and it was felt by this obscure woman in a distant village .

Here in the West, most people spend their days ridding themselves of discomfort and pain. We take medicines, we go to counseling, we read self-help books, all so we can escape a situation that God may actually want us to walk through. It's not that these solutions are bad in themselves, but we so often run to a solution so quickly that we may neglect discovering what God is trying to say in the process. One of my favorite books to use in preparing short-term mission teams is *When Helping Hurts* by Corbett and Fikkert, but the chiastic idea of "When hurting helps" might be a better concept to grasp. Hurting does help. This idea of the ministry of suffering is something we avoid, and rarely discuss. It's this suffering though that leads to brokenness.

Sometimes it's a lot easier to talk about other people's experiences, rather than my own. But this idea of the ministry of suffering is something I fully did not grasp for a vast majority of my life. I've seen lots of suffering though in my travels—the burn victim in LiJiang, the desperate mother in Heredia, the dying man in Kibera, and the orphan in Fengze whose cries went unanswered. But life for me has been pretty simple. I grew up in a loving home with two parents, ample support systems, people investing in my life, academic and athletic success, strong marriage, incredible kids, and financial and medical stability. I've come to realize that it really is a blessing to work with broken people in dysfunctional communities as it has not been something I easily identify with. However, in 2020 things changed for me. Not with the pandemic like you are probably anticipating. In 2020, I was diagnosed with an ascending aortic aneurysm that needed immediate surgical repair. I'm not a person who thinks a lot about death, but I can vividly remember sitting in my living room weeping as I listened to "I Can Only Imagine." Those first thoughts of death and missing out on decades of grandkids and memories left me in a puddle. Even the morning going into surgery, though I knew there were risks involved, I had confidence in my doctor, and had tons of prayer support. That moment being wheeled away though was surreal. I remember my wife's face trying to be strong for me, but both of us knew this could be our last time seeing each other on this side of heaven.

I woke up that night in ICU relieved—not because my heart was fixed, but because I was still alive. I was dehydrated, medicated, and disoriented, and I felt like I was suffering from a migraine—everything on my left was black. I had migraines before with blind spots and auras filtered throughout my field of vision but this was different as it wasn't a minor spot but an entire hemisphere in my eyes that was darkened. The doctor didn't seem too concerned as he said my dehydration probably caused it and by the time the morning rolled around I would probably be doing well. Well, the next morning did roll around and nothing changed. By late afternoon things were still the same. The following morning he had a therapist come in and do some tests on my eyesight and it was the first time I ever heard the word hemianopsia. I knew 'hemi' was a prefix for half, but no idea what the other part of that word meant. As the therapist explained to my wife and I, it looked like I had no vision in the left half of either eye. She wasn't sure why, but the MRI would soon reveal the cause. Going into a surgery of this magnitude, I knew there was a 1% chance of severe side effects, and I knew a stroke was one of those risks, but those things always happen to somebody else, not me. My life was ordered; it was neat. I was serving the Lord and my kids were all walking with Him, so why would I receive this? As I met with my neurologist a few days later, I still remember her words: "You're a man of faith, right? Well, you should be thankful because you had a large stroke that normally is something that takes a person's life or at least their ability to speak or walk. You're very fortunate that it lodged in your vision cortex. But, there's no medical history that this will get any better, but it probably won't get any worse." And my new life of being vision impaired started that day. I can't legally drive, I constantly run into doors and people, and some of those things that used to come so easily like catching a baseball are now quite difficult. I know this seems quite minor compared to people living in abject poverty or orphans with severe medical issues, but this gave me a glimpse into what suffering looks like and what it feels like. Even as my life found a new normal, it was only two months later that my family was camping. As I was carrying some garbage to the dumpster, I tripped over a storage bag and face-planted on a parking curb. Cracked teeth, three broken ribs, and a crack in the cement of a recently replaced knee accelerated my story of suffering a bit more. Once my body was ready for another major surgery, I went in to have the knee that I had replaced three years prior, replaced again. Physically I was a mess, but spiritually God was doing a deep work that I honestly don't think I could have learned unless I walked the path. 1 Peter 5:10 says, "And the God of all grace, who called you to his eternal glory in Christ, after you have suffered a little while, will himself restore you and make you strong, firm and steadfast." And that's what would give me hope. God hasn't forgotten me or abandoned me, in fact it was just the opposite—He was walking with me, leading me, and showing me his kindness and gentleness in a way I had not experienced before.

As we all try to follow Christ, sometimes it's those circumstances that change everything. And isn't that what we want? To see God transform and sanctify us into the person He wants us to be? I don't want to be the same person a year from now that I am today. I want to be more mature in my faith, have a deeper intimacy with the Savior, love people better, and have a deeper urgency for the spreading of the Gospel. But the guiding question may well be, "How do we get there?" The tendency is to turn spiritual maturity into an academic exercise rather than a spiritual exercise.

I was talking to a pastor in a foreign land about his discipleship process. He said he has a seventeen year process of books to read and Scripture to study. When I asked him how many have completed it, I knew the answer was zero before that word came out of his mouth. Most churches make their discipleship process an academic endeavor, rather than defining what they believe, learning to surrender, walking in God's power, and leaning into the brokenness in our lives. For the goal of these things is spiritual maturity.

Paul addresses this with the Ephesians:

> "So Christ himself gave the apostles, the prophets, the evangelists, the pastors and teachers, to equip his people for works of services, so that the body of Christ may be built up until we all reach unity in the faith and in the knowledge of the Son of God and become mature, attaining the whole measure of the fullness of Christ. Then we will no longer be infants, tossed back and forth by the waves, and blown here and there by every wind of teaching and by the cunning and craftiness of people in their deceitful scheming. Instead, speaking the truth in love, we will grow to become in every respect the mature body of him who is the head, that is, Christ."[1]

This is the maturity we should be striving for. Now, please don't hear what I am *not* saying. I am not saying that the study of God's word is in vain and we just need to grow in experiences. That's not it. But we can't just be an academic student or a hearer of the word. We need to live it out and have encounters with God. Ultimately, we need to walk with a limp. We need to wrestle with God. We need to get our hands so dirty in ministry that it begins to change how we think and how we live. In my life, the most seasoned men and women who are living out authentic faith, all walk with a limp. Somewhere in their past, they came to that place of brokenness that it becomes the new paradigm of how they see the world and their position in Christ.

As a mission pastor, I love the story of Jonathon Goforth. Because of my deep love for China, I've always been intrigued by Hudson Taylor, Gladys Aylward, and particularly Goforth. Goforth is especially fascinating because he walks with a limp. A limp that is not one I would desire, but one that has given him an understanding of faith that most of us have never seen. Goforth had five children die on the field, lost his possessions in a fire just two weeks into his journey, and again years later in a flood. He had to escape with his life during the Boxer Rebellion and ended his life blind. Yet his work in China was rooted in raising up indigenous leaders, planting churches and launching mission stations.[2] Like many of the great missionaries of the past two or three hundred years, he was intimately familiar with suffering—an extreme brokenness that created such a dependency on the Lord and a love for Him that he otherwise may never have discovered. And isn't that what we should desire—a deep dependency upon the Lord that comes from walking with a limp?

Wrapping up this first portion of Kung Fu Theology, let me take you back to the initial premise: we need to become like water. We need to become all things to all people so that we might win some. These four ideas are ones that we may never fully arrive at—to believe more deeply, surrender more fully, see God's power more clearly, and experience brokenness more intimately. But these are the non-negotiables for walking in maturity in your faith, and they are the cornerstones for beginning to build a life of demonstrating the person and character of Jesus to a lost and dying world that is far from Him. And that is the purpose of Kung Fu Theology.

Chapter 5
Discussion Questions

1. How do you think brokenness leads to a maturity of faith?

2. Who do you personally know who has experienced brokenness and how has that changed their walk with Christ?

3. How do you see people ridding themselves of discomfort and pain?

4. The phrase in the chapter is, "When hurting helps." Does it? If so, how?

5. Walking with a limp implies that you wrestled with God or have some 'war wounds' from your spiritual journey. How does this help your ministry to other people?

Part 2

Liquid Methodolgy

CHAPTER 6

Servant

"But do not use your freedom to indulge the flesh, rather, serve one another in love." Galatians 5:13

"You have not lived today until you have done something for someone who can never repay you." John Bunyan

It seems like the most significant experiences on most of my mission trips are the unscripted ones. Hours and hours of preparation go into creating a schedule, meetings, and trainings so that each day and each hour is maximized. But somewhere in the middle of each of these journeys are 'God moments' that I have to think He foreknew and arranged. I just needed to have eyes to see what was before me. One conversation was while standing on a watchtower on the Great Wall at Mutianyu was with a man who was at Tiananmen Square sharing his experience of what transpired that fateful night. Another was in the halls of Auschwitz with a woman whose grandmother died there and her photo was hanging on the wall. Another was in the backseat of a car driving through the Jordanian night with a man I had sat next to on the plane from Istanbul. Each one was unique in themselves, but compiled together, they paint a picture of the human soul that transcends culture and borders.

My time in Kenya was similar. The goal was to facilitate a training for fifty pastors about relational discipleship, but the farewell dinner revealed something about people that I just don't regularly see. A few years ago I met Augustine, a local pastor in the Murang'a area, and he was the facilitator for the trip so we got to spend a lot of time together, along with his wife, Zipporah, and his two children. Each morning we held the conference and then each evening we would be back at the local inn sharing a meal with a few of the leaders in the area. The last night was quite celebratory to conclude a meaningful conference as well as sealing a fast-developing friendship. Around the table were the three of us from the states, Augustine and Zipporah, our partner from Uganda, as well as another couple who had significant roles in serving at the conference. As with each trip, my goal is never to bring any supplies home as there is always someone who is in need that could make better use of whatever we still had. Each of the couples around the table lived quite simply by any standard. They faithfully served their community, but pastoring in poor areas was a sacrifice in multiple ways—materially being one of those. After exchanging the gifts we brought, we then gave out the remaining supplies of buckets, towels, and games that we had used as props for ice breakers at the conference. I gave about eight sets of each to Zipporah having invested in their family, church, and school in a variety of ways. I didn't think too much about it as I handed them over to her, since to me it seemed like a normal gesture. I returned to my seat at the other end of the table to enjoy the rest of the chicken and rice oblivious to what was happening at her end of the table. Zipporah took half of what she had and handed it to the other woman saying, "When you're blessed, you bless." Those words echoed in my mind the entire night. I had been to Zipporah's home and seen firsthand the simplicity in which she lived. I walked the grounds of the school where she taught and saw the multiple needs there. And I saw the church with the dirt floor and missing windows. Yet, she took what she had and gave it away.

That's what Kung Fu Theology looks like lived out. Yes, it's that simple. Bruce Lee's words, "You put water into a cup, it becomes a cup. You put it in a teapot, it becomes a teapot," looks just like what I saw at the dinner table. Zipporah is characterized by possessing the solid elements of theology, and she captures the first trait of Liquid Methodology—the heart of a servant.

Living out faith in a tangible way is rooted in having the heart of a servant. It seems trivial to replay the story from Scripture, but sometimes we make faith so complex we lose sight of the simple truths that Jesus taught and lived out over and over again. As James and John come to Jesus in Mark 10, they ask Jesus to sit at his side in glory. As the other disciples become indignant with them, Jesus says, "Whoever wants to become great among you must be your servant, and whoever wants to be first must be slave of all. For even the Son of Man did not come to be served, but to serve, and to give his life as a ransom for many."[1]

Don't miss this: Jesus. Came. To. Serve. He served at the wedding feast, he washed his disciples' feet, and cared for those who were sick. I always wonder what John meant in the closing lines of his Gospel: "Jesus did many other things as well. If every one of them were written down, I suppose that even the whole world would not have room for the books that would be written."[2] I want to be cautious of creating things that are extra-biblical in guessing what those "many other things" were, but it's not hard to make a logical guess based on the character of Jesus and what we know to be true about him. He probably loved the marginalized over and over again like he did the leper; he probably nurtured the child who was sick;

he probably spoke kind words to the women who felt they had no value. That's just who he is—he is known by how he loved people well and served them. So how are you known? Would people describe you as a servant? Would they describe you as one who puts the needs of others above your own? It's my hope in these chapters of the methodology of faith that we wouldn't be so quick in how to encourage others to live this way, but we would look in the mirror first. Are we asking people to do things that we don't do ourselves? This has nothing to do with your position, or your standing, or your status. This has to do with your heart. Jesus asked the same thing of the most influential pastors in your area, as well as the person sitting in the back row of the church—to be a servant of all. Paul, who was probably the most significant person in the foundation of the church, wrote, "In humility value others above yourselves, not looking to your own interests but each of you to the interests of others."[3]

Paul is an interesting case study in how he viewed himself and his position in Christ. Looking chronologically through Paul's life, it is easy to see the transformation that took place in his life and one that I hope is evident in my own as I get to know Christ. Paul wrote 1 Corinthians in about 55 A.D. and wrote, "For I am the least of the apostles and do not even deserve to be called an apostle because I persecuted the church of God."[4] As Paul journeys with Christ, it's about five years later that he writes Ephesians in 60-62 A.D. and says, "I am less than the least of all the Lord's people."[5] In five years, Paul viewed himself as moving from the least of the apostles to the least of all the Christ followers. Then about two years later, in 62-64 A.D., Paul wrote to Timothy, "Christ Jesus came into the world to save sinners—of whom I am the worst."[6] It is during this time when he writes to the Philippians that he says:

> "If someone else thinks they have reasons to put confidence in the flesh, I have more: circumcised on the eighth day, of the people of Israel, of the tribe of Benjamin, a Hebrew of Hebrews; in regard to the law, a Pharisee; as for zeal, persecuting the church; as for righteousness based on the law, faultless. But whatever were gains to me I now consider loss for the sake of Christ. What is more, I consider everything a loss because of the surpassing worth of knowing Christ Jesus my Lord, for whose sake I have lost all things. I consider them garbage, that I may gain Christ."[7]

Paul has many valid reasons to elevate himself, but as he grows closer to Christ, he becomes more and more humble in the process. Rather than exalting himself as he grows in influence with the church, Paul takes on the same attitude that Christ had as he washes feet and tells his followers he came to serve and not to be served. Paul comes to the end of himself. He has reason to put confidence in the flesh, but as he grows in his understanding of the saving grace of Christ, he becomes a servant to all.

Living out this Kung Fu Theology begins with having the heart of a servant. And having a liquid mentality changes how this is lived out. Often we just want to serve our families, or our church, but Christ calls us to much more than that. He calls us to serve our neighbor and the stranger. In theory, it sounds simple. For me, it's not always that simple. So often I have a list of tasks to accomplish, or an agenda driving me, that I don't stop for the person in front of me. How can I expect to reach people with the love of Jesus when I walk right by them or put my own agenda above those whom God may be putting in my path? But this is where spiritual maturity is developed and where it is lived out—in being a servant.

When I read Scripture, sometimes living out faith like Paul or Peter or John seems so unattainable. Often I do better with contemporary examples that have the heart of those Biblical characters, but who do it in a culture I can identify with. Let me present two people to you—one you have probably heard of, and one that you won't meet on this side of heaven.

Several years ago I had the privilege of traveling to Weifang, China. Weifang is another one of the hundreds of cities in China, with multiple millions of people, that a vast majority of people around the world have never heard of. As I walked out of the train station, this could have been any of the dozens of large cities in China I have traveled. Crowds of people met me at the doors of the station. Floods of Chinese people exiting with one Caucasian, six-foot-four man looming above the others, drawing a lot of instant attention. The taxi drivers shouted the one word of English they knew, "Taxi!" Middle-aged men in sweat-soaked dress shirts approached with the words, "You want ride?" And my job was to find the one Chinese person I had never met who was to be my host that week—David. Having been in those situations multiple times, I learned to exit the station and stand in a visible spot and let him find me. Fortunately, it didn't take long for an unknown man to come up and ask, "Are you Steve?" There's always a sense of relief for me at this point as I'm never sure what I would do if my host failed to show. Plus I would guess there is a strange sense of pride for my host walking away with the only foreigner in a crowd of several thousand Chinese people who live in an area that rarely, if ever, saw foreigners. So rare, that I spent four days there and never saw a single foreigner among the nine million people within the city limits.

Even though my purpose for the trip was to establish an educational center in the city, I had one personal reason of why I always wanted to go to Weifang. We all have heroes of the faith and one of mine has always been Eric Liddell—the topic of the Academy Award-winning Best Picture of 1981, *Chariots of Fire.* Born of Scottish missionary parents, his claim to fame was running in the 1924 Summer Olympics where he refused to run heats for his best race, the 100 meters, because they were held on a Sunday. Though this was what made him famous, this isn't what made him great. After the Olympics, he moved to China to serve as a missionary. As the Japanese forces started moving into China, Eric sent his family back to England, and he was placed in the Weihsien Internment Camp in Weifang. Dr. David Michell, who was one of the children in the camp, writes of 'Uncle Eric:'

> "Not only did Eric Liddell organize sports and recreation, through his time in internment camp he helped many people through teaching and tutoring. He gave special care to the older people, the weak, and the ill, to whom the conditions in camp were very trying. He was always involved in the Christian meetings which were a part of camp life. Despite the squalor of the open cesspools, rats, flies and disease in the

crowded camp, life took on a very normal routine, though without the faithful and cheerful support of Eric Liddell, many people would never have been able to manage."[8]

Then in 1944, Winston Churchill approved a prisoner exchange and, since he was a famous athlete, Eric was chosen to leave. But instead of receiving his own granted safety, he gave it up and offered his place to a pregnant woman instead.[9] Though this part of the story is disputed, the reputation of Liddell was enough for people to believe it as true. This humble man, who was once a world-famous athlete, served out his final years of life in a camp where his audience was his fellow prisoners, and he lived out those days serving these people until his eventual death within the camp walls.

In Weifang, there is a small monument commemorating his life, and the camp is still standing at the present site of the Weifang No. 2 Middle School. David drove me there that day. I walked the grounds and looked in the small rooms asking God to put that same heart Liddell had, in me—to walk away from the enticement of the world and set my heart and mind on the things above. To serve people humbly. To love the stranger. To make life bearable for others.

I stood at the camp gate longer than most people would. But since no one else was there, David permitted me to take my time. Somewhere amid the cicadas chirping and the summer humidity bearing down on the hot concrete, I understood more at that moment what living life as a servant meant than I had in years—a solitary man who gave up the comfort of the world to serve those he had never met and willingly laid his life down. Understanding it was one thing; living it out is my constant challenge. And more than likely, the challenge you are facing too.

Clay Floch is a man you will most likely not meet on this side of heaven. He grew up in a nearby farming community in Eastern Washington and quietly served the Lord while he and his wife raised two boys. In the world's terms, Clay is quite ordinary. He works hard, and loves well. In 2001 while his two boys, who were about both about twenty years old and high-achieving athletes, were out ocean fishing with their cousin and grandfather off the coast of Washington, their boat capsized, costing all four of them their lives in the cold water. As would be expected, grief hit Clay and Jewel hard losing their only two children. The years slowly passed, and it was in early 2008 that Clay reached out to me. Clay's words were profound that night, but would grow more so over the years: "Ever since we lost our boys, life has been pretty meaningless. I was wondering if you would consider taking us to China on the summer mission trip to the orphanage, as I need to do something to bring purpose back to my life. I don't have any special skills but I know how to work hard and how to love." Six months later, Clay and his wife, Jewel, were on the plane heading to Langfang, China. Lord willing, in my life I will have about 30,000 days to live, but June 20, 2008 will be forever remembered.

The day started like most of our days at Shepherd's Field in Langfang—a Pop Tart, a team meeting, and off to do various jobs that would help serve the 100 or so special-needs orphans and dozens of nannies. I remember Clay's job that day as I worked part of the day beside him. We were up in the attic of one of the children's homes removing supplies and taking it to the adjacent home. The attic was just what you would expect as there was one tiny vent in the corner with 100 degree temps and 90% humidity. By the end of the first thirty minutes, we had both sweat through our t-shirts and still had a few hours to go. I made up some excuse to go check on the team, and Clay continued to outwork young men half his age.

Each night, we would board our bus and go to the local hot pot restaurant or noodle shop. It was literally our first night there and everyone was anticipating their first authentic Chinese meal. As Jewel came down the stairs to catch the bus, she tripped on the bottom step and was in immediate pain. If anyone deserved to go out that night, it was Clay since he worked all day in the attic. But Clay also knew that staying back with his wife was more important than his first attempt at chopsticks. As I walked out the door, Clay was on the couch holding an ice pack on his wife's ankle.

All through dinner I felt badly for Clay, as I really wanted him to have an experience that would bring some type of deep healing. As we walked back into the orphanage after dinner, I saw just what God had in mind. The two of them were still on the coach, but with them was a teenage girl named Stacey. I knew Stacey from the previous year's visit. She was an orphan who had aged out of the adoption process but stayed at Shepherd's Field where she could heal from the severe burns she had over much of her body from a childhood accident. Clay and Jewel could hardly get the words out before the tears poured out. For the past two hours they had talked with Stacey, who captivated their hearts and by the end of the evening, they were convinced they should try to make a special request to adopt her and bring her to Spokane. While I was eating a hot pot that would make my Sichuan friends proud, God was ministering to their hearts in a way that was completely unscripted...at least in our eyes, but I think the Lord knew.

During the months that followed, Clay found out that the Chinese government would not permit them to adopt Stacey because of her age or even foster her while receiving medical care. And what happened next is what will make Clay a forever hero in my eyes. Since they couldn't adopt Stacey, they let her 'adopt' them. Within a few months, they sold everything and moved to China to serve at the orphanage alongside Stacey. Most missionaries I know, or read about, are either great evangelists, community development specialists, medically trained, or business developers. But Clay went because he "knew how to work hard and love others." That was it. He worked hard and loved well. He loved hundreds of orphans, dozens of nannies, and many staff people. The other incredible part of the story is that Clay and Jewel ended up adopting two little girls—one with spina bifida and another with brittle bone disease. It's these 'God moments' that were unscripted when they departed, but ones that the Lord had in mind all along.

And that's what serving well looks like. Clay became all things to all people in a little town in northeast China so that he might win some. Being a servant doesn't take an incredible gifting or talent; it just takes someone who is willing to say yes to Jesus' call to, "Follow me and I will make you a fisher of men,"[10] to follow him, to be changed by him, and to be on mission with him. And that's Kung Fu Theology.

Chapter 6
Discussion Questions

1. Who do you personally know who models being a servant? What is it that stands out?

2. It is sometimes easier to find examples of serving in third world cultures, but what are three or four easy ways to serve in Western culture?

3. Serving sometimes requires giving of your time, talent, and treasures. Which is the most difficult, and which is the easiest for you and why?

4. We often use the verbiage of finding a place inside and outside of your local church to serve. How are you doing both?

5. What is it that stirs your heart in the brokenness we see around us? Who in your area is doing something about it, and what are they doing? Is there a place for you to help?

CHAPTER 7

Faith Not Fear

*"Be strong and courageous. Do not be afraid;
do not be discouraged, for the Lord your
God will be with you wherever you go."
Joshua 1:9*

*"If the Lord be with us, we have no cause of
fear. His eye is upon us, His arm over us, His
ear open to our prayer—His grace sufficient,
His promise unchangeable. Under His
protection, though the path of duty should
lie through fire and water, we may cheerfully
and confidently pursue it." John Newton*

I love Chapter 7. This is the chapter that begins
to put the rubber to the road and begins to answer
the question, "What do you do with all of this?" The
solid principles of theology are foundational building
blocks of faith, and the idea of being a servant is the
preparation of putting this into action. Having a catchy

title like *Kung Fu Theology* is really pointless if being and making disciples is just an academic exercise of someone's deep thoughts about Christianity. I think back to my days pitching at Washington State University and the hours and hours of practice we put in—throwing bullpens, long toss, fielding drills, strategy talks, lifting, and lots of running. Each of those things are extremely valuable in and of themselves, but if I had never gotten into a game, I honestly don't know what use they would have been. I vividly remember those winter afternoons fielding ground balls on the frozen turf of Martin Stadium where the football games were held, while my friends who chose to go to school in Arizona were putting on sunscreen. But there was the knowledge that each of those repetitions would pay dividends when Oregon State or Washington came to town.

And faith is similar. Hours of prayer, studying scripture, worshipping, and accountability groups were all designed to move us from being a spectator to being a participant. We weren't designed to sit on the sidelines—we are invited to get in the game and put our faith into action. This chapter is the first transition to that. We know the solid principles, we develop our servant's heart, and we start moving towards "becoming all things to all people so that by all possible means I might win some."[1] But, sometimes it's not so easy. I remember the first time I shared the gospel with a close friend back in 1985 at the Montlake Bridge on the University of Washington campus. I was passionate, but I was scared. What if she asked me questions I didn't know the answer to? What if she rejected me and our friendship? What if she said no? I realize that those fears are normal, but they can't be reasons for not engaging.

My wife, Carrie, has always had a few taglines that became part of our family over the years. "Faith, not Fear" was one that helped anchor us in a lot of big decisions over the years. I know she didn't coin the phrase, but I'm giving her credit because I've heard it in her voice so many times that I can't imagine anyone else saying it. Every time she said it, I would feel like I was at the top step of the dugout heading to the mound, with my coach slapping me on the back saying, "You got this!" And this is the point that Kung Fu Theology becomes fully liquid. Throughout scripture, the people God used walked by faith and not by fear. Daniel was told not to bow, Rahab was told to hang a scarlet thread, and Benaiah was told to go down into a pit. Ordinary people, doing extraordinary things, because they were not paralyzed by fear.

Charles Blondin, in 1859, did something that no one thought possible when he crossed Niagara Falls on a tightrope. His feats became famous across Europe and the West, so much so that thousands of people would come out to watch. On one day, he spoke to the crowd,

"Who thinks I can walk across this rope without falling to my death?" The crowd cheered their approval and off Blondin went to one end and then back to where he started. Again he challenged the crowd, "Who thinks I can push a wheelbarrow across the rope?" The crowd was still cheering as Blondin walked across and then back with a wheelbarrow in front of him. By now, the crowd was in a frenzy. "Who thinks I can push a man in the wheelbarrow across the rope and back?" Everyone, feeling quite confident, chanted Blondin's name in support. "So," Blondin said, "who will get in?" And the crowd was silent and motionless.[2]

This is how we often live our lives. We believe that God is who he says he is. We believe God's word is true. And we believe that God empowers us. Yet, we won't get into His wheelbarrow. We often stand frozen in fear because of the unknown in front of us. In the West, we get paralyzed because we have become accustomed to the "as soon as" disease. As soon as I finish school; as soon as I get married; as soon as I get a home; as soon as I get a promotion; as soon as the kids are grown; as soon as the kids move out; as soon as I retire; as soon as….you fill in the blank. And as a result, we often don't do the things that God has put on our heart.

I'm sitting in the corner at Panera as I write this chapter, and it's honestly not fair of me to project that you have fear and I don't. Let me tell you a story that may be of some encouragement:

I've read Randy Alcorn's book, *Safely Home*, multiple times. With the deep burden I have for the Chinese people and the brokenness I have for unreached and unengaged people, this book is the perfect marriage of the two. And of course, reading it in the comfort of my own home makes it feel more like a true work of fiction than the reality of what is truly happening with the persecuted church in China. Most Christians want a story that they can tell, especially Christians in the West, because most of our stories of persecution are someone ridiculing us on social media, or an elected official speaking out against the church. Several years ago, I was in a remote area of China trying to establish some relationships of how we might be able to partner together in order to promote the spreading of the gospel and develop the beginning of a disciple-making movement. Through a friend of a friend of a friend, I found myself at a street barbecue with a man I'll call Liang and my friend who is a translator. This luncheon date was arranged secretly and I was surprised Liang agreed to it, as he was very influential in his region. As we ate and got to know each other, it was quite apparent to me that this man had a significant impact. He had seen the church planting movement spread into third and fourth generation churches, but he also had been jailed multiple times. Soon after we ate, we began our walk to our next destination with him. I'm sure there was a more direct way to get there, but I followed his lead as we went up and down alleyways, inside shops, and eventually I realized that his path was to avoid detection and avoid being followed. He could quickly disappear into the mass of people, but having a 6'4" white American man with him would draw attention, this time unwanted. After nearly thirty minutes of walking, we came to a four-story building that seemed to be a vacated hotel. Everything was torn up, and there were no visible signs of any recent guests, and there were no people around. As with many Chinese buildings, it is often difficult to discern what the practical use is because they tend to be cookie cutters of one another so they can go up quickly. It is just recently that architectural design began to be commonplace in the major East Coast cities of Shanghai and Hong Kong. We walked up the staircase to the third-floor and down to the end of the hallway. As we entered, there were already seven or eight people prepared for our arrival. This would've been a typical hotel room, but there was no furniture except for two dozen small plastic stools around the perimeter of the room. Even as Liang introduced me, he spoke in hushed tones and all the replies were at the same volume. Over the next thirty minutes, people came in ones and twos into the room until there were about 25 people crammed into the small space. Liang introduced me and my translator told me that the next part would be entirely in Chinese and I could either observe or pray along with them. Over the course of my forty years of being a Christ follower, I've been in churches that had organs and choirs, and those that had drums and fog machines. But I have never been in a worship setting like I was in that room. One of the women sitting to my left took the position of worship leader. As she was silhouetted against the window, I couldn't make out her expressions, but there was a heavy sense of holiness in that room. In barely a whisper, she started singing a song in Chinese and the people soon joined. I sat quietly on my stool and tried to absorb as much as I could. The twenty-five voices together were no louder than a single whisper, but I imagine they sounded louder in heaven than an auditorium full of people back home. I'm not sure if you have ever been in an area of the world that is antagonistic toward the gospel, but worship in those places is different. By the end of the first stanza, the tears were flowing from most of the people and they were all in a posture of deep humility and reverence. It's evident that this gathering of believers is much more than singing a few songs; it's about worshipping the God who has rescued them from a deep place of separation from Himself. It is so hard to capture this atmosphere for people. I recently was in a social media conversation with a Christ-follower in my city who was trying to convince people that you don't have to go to church, that you don't have to fellowship corporately. But until you experience a room like this, similar to the ones I've seen in the Middle East, you may never encounter this kind of intimacy on this side of heaven.

The worship went on like this for well over an hour. And the voices never raised. There were moments of silence, but this choir of whispers was a prelude to what I hope heaven will be like. Liang then took the lead and started speaking to them in a similar hushed voice. I could glance at his Bible and knew he was in one of the Gospels by where his Bible was open. He was just picking up his intensity when a knock from the door interrupted his words. Every head turned and Liang's eyes were unblinking saucers as we all knew what it would mean if it was the local PSB. For me, my heart froze, and I quickly played through what this would mean for me. Would I be sent home and forever flagged from entering my favorite country? Would I be arrested? Would I be beaten? Would my new friends be tortured?

The man nearest the door stood to open it. There in the doorway was a young woman who greeted everyone with smiles. A collective exhale was laced with relief. Apparently this woman was known and must have just been late. As the door shut, my wife's words surfaced from somewhere deep within me, "Faith, not fear."

For us in the West, "Faith, not fear" usually doesn't wear this face. We don't fear physical harm. We don't fear imprisonment. We don't fear that we will lose everything just for following this Jesus. But we are often still paralyzed by fear when we move from being a hearer of the word, to being a doer of the word. And the big question surrounding this is "Why?" Why are we so afraid in the West to walk in full obedience? Why are we so hesitant in reaching people outside of our circle who are different than us? Using the metaphor woven throughout this book, why do we want to live in the solid and not in the liquid? Honestly, I think it's for a few reasons.

First, we have learned not to walk by faith. Even though Paul wrote, "For we live by faith, not by sight,"[3] when it comes down to it, we usually don't. We structure and plan our lives to create comfort, remove stressors, and package it in such a way that we can anticipate what the next week or month or year will hold. This is a difficult balance because even in Proverbs it says, "In their hearts humans plan their course, but the Lord establishes their steps."[4] Having a plan is not wrong, but when it's at the expense of listening and following the Lord, we should reconsider how we live. Francis Chan may have captured it best for our contemporary society as I remember him asking a question at a conference where he was speaking: "What are you doing right now that requires faith?" He then challenged us to think of some area in our life that was directly affected by living by faith. As I looked around me at the conference, I realized I was surrounded by people who probably were living the same way I did. I remember Chan saying that for most of us, our lives are characterized by comfort. I knew that was not what God called me to—a life of comfort. But rather, He called me to such a dependency on Him that I would be in trouble if he doesn't come through.

Second, we are often afraid of what God may ask of us. What if He asks us to sell everything and move to Africa? What if He asks us to quit our job and pursue a different calling? Because we are so afraid of what God may ask, we end up putting ourselves in positions where we don't need to listen to Him, and we crowd out our lives with noise and busyness so there is no time to listen when that opportunity may arise. I would guess if you are reading this book, you have been in multiple prayer situations—alone, dinner tables, small groups, things like that. But, in those times, how much of it is spent listening to what God may want to say to us? Scripture is very clear when it says, "This is what the Lord says, he who made the earth, the Lord who formed it and established it—the Lord is his name: 'Call to me and I will answer you and tell you great and unsearchable things you do not know.'"[5] But there should be such security in knowing that God loves us and sees in us things we may not see in ourselves. And what greater privilege is there than to talk to the God who put the planets into motion and the stars into place and who wants to speak to us.

Finally, and this is one that I know I struggle with also—we're selfish and when it comes down to it, we want to live our lives on our terms. And this may be the point where we really have to take an honest look in the mirror again. If we really believe that eternity awaits those that follow Christ, and God has such a better life planned for people, then why is there no urgency in sharing this news with as many people as possible? The magician and atheist, Penn Jillette, explaining why he doesn't respect people who don't proselytize said, "I don't respect that at all. If you believe there's a heaven and hell and people could be going to hell or not getting eternal life or whatever, and you think that it's not really worth telling them this because it would make it socially awkward, and atheists who think that people shouldn't proselytize—'just leave me alone, keep your religion to yourself.' How much do you have to hate somebody to not proselytize? How much do you have to hate somebody to believe that everlasting life is possible and not tell them that?"[6] Whether our fear is that we don't want to offend, or we are too busy, or like Jonah, we just don't want to, we really need to reconsider and search our heart as to why that is.

We have the greatest news in the world and we are commanded to go share it. Yet, many of us don't.

So what do you do with all of this? Whether you classify it as fear or busyness, or just plain old apathy or selfishness, how do you begin to move to living out this faith? Honestly, it starts with baby steps. Faith is like a muscle that needs to be exercised and strengthened, and, as we develop it, we can carry more and more. As faith is exercised, we can look backward and see how God was faithful again and again, which will then be a catalyst for taking greater steps of faith. God encouraged this from a long time ago when the Israelites crossed the Jordan river into the promised land. Joshua says, "Each of you is to take up a stone on his shoulder, according to the number of the tribes of the Israelites, to serve as a sign among you. In the future when your children ask you, 'What do these stones mean?' Tell them that the flow of the Jordan was cut off before the ark of the covenant of the Lord. When it crossed the Jordan, the waters of the Jordan were cut off. These stones are to be a memorial to the people of Israel forever."[7]

Being able to look back and see God's faithfulness strengthens the faith muscle. I can look back and see how God prompted me to take small steps of faith so that when big steps were needed, my faith muscle was trained and I could look back at a long history of His faithfulness. As I moved from being a teenager who decided to talk about Jesus in my high school graduation speech, to adoption, to quitting jobs, to moving houses, it all centered around wanting to do what God was asking of me at that moment in that season. Was I fearful during those times? Of course. But it wasn't paralyzing. I had seen God's faithfulness in those moments when I knew I would be in trouble if He didn't show up. But what I have noticed as I have walked this journey is that I am able to combat the fear that the enemy and the world want to cause me by having a few things in place. First, I try to pray regularly and talk to God about these things. This happens on afternoon runs, on drives to work, and the morning time set apart for Him. I know that the sheep know the shepherd's voice and He wants to speak, so I need to create moments in the day where I am ready to listen. Next, being able to combat fear came from reading the Bible consistently. The more I learned about the character of God and about the evidence of His faithfulness from the beginning, it began to gird me up so that I could choose faith over fear. Another piece I had in place was an intimate relationship with my wife knowing that we were in this together and I have learned to trust her discernment in our decision making. God didn't always bring us to the same decision at the same time, but we have learned to walk in step together through each deci-sion which has made choosing faith over fear much easier. In addition, I have always had some men in my life who closely followed the Lord who I could share with. Hours running with my friend, Dick, sitting in my office with Jay, hanging out in Alex's classroom, having coffee with Paul, and office visits with LeRoy, were all moments that God spoke into my life through them. All of these structures have built a framework where choosing to obey became the only option. And as Carrie and I made hard decisions, my faith muscle began to grow so that fear would not win out and I could do what God was asking of me.

Rather than ending this chapter with another story about overcoming fear or a personal testimony of living this out, I want to take you back to scripture to one of the first verses I ever memorized and has been so critical in my faith journey. As Paul is writing to the Romans, he says, "Therefore, I urge you brothers, in view of God's mercy, to offer your bodies as a living sacrifice, holy and pleasing to God—this is your true and proper worship. Do not conform to the pattern of this world, but be transformed by the renewing of your mind. Then you will be able to test and approve what God's will is—his good pleasing and perfect will."[8] There is so much in this verse that can drive this idea of living by faith and not fear. So often we want to conform to the world because it is enticing.

It is satisfying to the flesh, though God wants to give you something better that is satisfying to the soul. Sometimes God calls us to do what is not normal, or what would not make sense to people in the world. For instance, why would I leave a teaching job I love, where I was earning good money with good benefits at a good school where I was teaching my favorite classes with summer's off, to take a job in vocational ministry for 60% of the pay and no benefits? Or why would we sell a house that we loved? Or leave a different job to spend a year looking for work while I had five kids at home to provide for? The answer—God said so. As we tried diligently to not conform to the world, we were able to hear God's voice clearly and discern what He was asking of us. It wasn't easy, but it became easier as we grew in our spiritual maturity. And for my wife and I, the words of Isaiah are so true, "Do not turn your ear to the left or to the right, but listen to the voice behind you saying, this is the way, walk in it."[9] And that's Kung Fu Theology.

Chapter 7
Discussion Questions

1. What stirs up fear in you?

2. How do you combat it?

3. What is something that God revealed to you that fear caused you to not fully obey it?

4. As you look backward in your life, what are 3-4 incidents where you saw God come through, and it has strengthened your faith?

5. What is God asking of you right now which causes you to wrestle with faith and fear?

CHAPTER 8

See

"For the Lord sees not as man sees; man looks on the outward appearance, but the Lord looks on the heart." 1 Samuel 16:7

"What does love look like? It has the hands to help others. It has the feet to hasten to the poor and needy. It has eyes to see misery and want. It has the ears to hear the sighs and sorrows of men. That is what love looks like." Augustine

In the Gospel of Mark, there is a story about Jesus' travels:

"Then they came to Jericho. As Jesus and his disciples, together with a large crowd, were leaving the city, a blind man, Bartimaeus (which means "son of Timaeus"), was sitting by the roadside begging. When he heard that it was Jesus of Nazareth, he began to shout, 'Jesus, Son of David, have mercy on me!' Many rebuked him and told him to be quiet, but he shouted all the more, 'Son of David, have mercy on me!' Jesus stopped and said, 'Call him.' So they called to the blind man, 'Cheer up! On your feet! He's calling you.' Throwing his cloak aside, he jumped to his feet and came to Jesus. 'What do you want me to do for you?' Jesus asked him. The blind man said, 'Rabbi, I want to see.' 'Go,' said Jesus, 'your faith has healed you.' Immediately he received his sight and followed Jesus along the road."[1]

For several years this has been my favorite Bible story—seven verses nestled in the narrative of Jesus' life. And there are so many sermon illustrations in these few verses. From a literary point of view, I love how Mark juxtaposes this passage with verse 36 when Jesus asked James and John the exact same question, "What do you want me to do for you?" They give the answer of how they want to sit at the right and left hand of Jesus in the heavens. Then ten verses later, Jesus asked Bartimaeus, a poor beggar sitting on the side of the road, what he would want Jesus to do for him. I can picture this scene as I'm sure most of you can too, because we've lived that scene. We've all walked down the busy sidewalk and seen a beggar on the side of the road asking for change, and I'm guessing many of us have walked right by him. I've justified it by thinking I have a busy schedule, or I don't trust what the person will do with the money, but I've also spent many days approaching people sitting on the proverbial side of the road—and I walked right past. But not Jesus. Jesus stopped. While those around Jesus were telling the man to be quiet, Jesus stopped. And Bartimaeus' answer to the question is much more profound than we realize. Most of the time we just read this and think it's a blind beggar who just wants to physically see. But I think it's much deeper than that. I, too, want to see. For Bartimaeus, this was the last time Jesus would ever walk through his city, and this was his moment to have an encounter with the Lord, so he threw everything aside and cried out even more for Jesus to have mercy on him. In those four words, "I want to see," he captures the next part of the liquid methodology of Kung Fu Theology—seeing.

Having the heart of a servant and living by faith and not fear are the first principles, but now we need to see with different eyes—eyes that look outward and not inward. At the beginning of so many days while I spend time praying, I find myself going through my calendar and praying about each specific meeting, task, or activity that I had during that day. What I'm trying to learn how to do instead, is to ask the Lord to open my eyes and give me his vision to see people around me through His view and not my own. This part is critical because this is where ministry often happens best. It happens in the spontaneous; it happens in the unscheduled; it happens when we stop for the person in front of us. And it's not always just on the sidewalk downtown, sometimes it's on Sunday morning in our own churches. Sometimes the best time of ministry happens right in the foyer by initiating a simple conversation. And most often, it comes from looking around the environment to see where God may want you to go. For me, the most common places seem to be in the grocery stores, in the waiting rooms, and at my kids sporting events. Those times, when there may be five to ten minutes standing or sitting next to someone, and instead of talking about rising prices or last week's scores, a simple intentional conversation can open a door to much deeper spiritual conversations. I have to think that Jesus did the same as he walked from place to place, so why can't I do it sitting in the doctor's waiting room?

Let me tell you a story. Just recently I went to Honduras to assess a ministry that was working with nursing students in one of the rural towns. On Wednesday morning, we took the sixteen students and went to the city square which is where a surprising number of people were hanging out sitting in the shade.

We broke up our group into four smaller ones, and each went to a different corner of the square to ask people if they would like some basic medical care. The young women would then take some vitals, ask a series of questions, provide some help, and then always end by praying for their patient. For the first hour, each of my nurses were able to meet with two or three people in the park. But while this was happening, my attention was constantly directed towards a man sitting across the street watching all of this happen. And this man was, well, let's just say, a bit harder looking than the others. But from a distance, he sat and watched all of this happen in front of him. Before we departed for the square earlier that morning, we prayed for the Lord to draw our attention to those who needed help. Eventually, I grabbed two of the young nurses and we walked across the street to this man. Even though I don't speak Spanish, it was clearly evident that this man was hurting emotionally more than he was hurting physically. Our conversation went on for about twenty minutes until he asked the three of us if we would pray for him. He had told the story of how his family left, he lost his job, and was pretty hopeless at this point. We spent the next fifteen or twenty minutes just ministering to him. No vitals were taken. No medical care was given. But these young women gave hope to the hopeless which was probably the greatest cure of all at that moment.

And that's what seeing is all about. It sounds so simple yet so often we never do it. Several years ago the Christian artist, Brandon Heath, released a song called, "Give Me Your Eyes." He wrote:

Give me Your eyes for just one second
Give me Your eyes so I can see
Everything that I keep missin'
Give me Your love for humanity
Give me Your arms for the broken-hearted
The ones that are far beyond my reach
Give me Your heart for the ones forgotten
Give me Your eyes so I can see. [2]

Do you ever pray to see the world around you with God's eyes? It really has been amazing that during the days I have prayed this prayer, God has changed the course of my interactions with people. Opportunities that never seemed to have existed now appear all around me. People that used to fade into the walls now seem to be in my path, and those I may have walked right by, I now stop for. And all throughout the gospels, this seemed to be how Jesus lived.

Looking through the Gospel of Mark, it reveals a lot of how Jesus saw the need: "After feeding the 5000, Jesus sent the disciples off ahead of him to Bethsaida while he went up on the mountain to pray."[3] Picture the humanity of Jesus in this moment—at the start of the day, he told the disciples to come with him to a quiet place and get some rest. Yet, the people followed and Jesus had compassion on them and he began to teach them...all day. Then the people were hungry, so Jesus fed them. And not a small crowd mind you, more than likely it was somewhere between 15,000 – 20,000 people. Then he sent the disciples off and he went to a quiet place to pray. But while he was there, "He saw the disciples straining at the oars, because the wind was against them. Shortly before dawn he went out to them."[3] So Jesus started the day needing some rest, preached to several thousands of people, prayed all night, and then he saw a need, and went to meet it. But that was who Jesus was.

I wish that was always my heart. Sometimes I see the need and choose not to meet it. Sometimes I see the need and hope someone else meets it. And sometimes I don't see the need because I don't look for it. Yet the bigger question is, why do I choose to not look for the needs around me? Could be selfishness, could be pride, could be apathy, or it could be I just don't want to get involved. But, that is not what God calls us to. Earlier in this book, I shared the word 'Hineni.' When Abraham, and Moses, and Samuel, and Isaiah said, "Here am I," the word they were saying was Hineni, a Hebrew word with the translated meaning, "Whatever you are about to ask, I am already in agreement with it." But there is one time in Scripture that God says *"Hineni"* to us. Imagine God saying, "Steve, whatever you are about to ask, I am already in agreement with it"? In Isaiah 58:

> "Is not this the kind of fasting I have chosen: to loose the chains of injustice and untie the cords of the yoke, to set the oppressed free and break every yoke? Is it not to share your food with the hungry and to provide the poor wanderer with shelter when you see the naked, to clothe them, and not to turn away from your own flesh and blood? Then your light will break forth like the dawn, and your healing will quickly appear; then your righteousness[a] will go before you, and the glory of the Lord will be your rear guard. Then you will call, and the Lord will answer; you will cry for help, and he will say: 'Here am I.'"[4]

As I see and meet the need of those around me, God says to me, "Whatever you are about to ask, I am already in agreement with it." This is an incredible thought, but it is reflective of where your heart needs to be when you are seeing the need around you. As I feed the hungry, shelter the wanderer, and clothe

the naked, it reveals that my heart is in a place of submission to the Lord. And that is the answer to why I often don't see the need around me. It's because my own heart is not in a place of submission to the Lord and is focused on myself and my own wants and desires. But the reward of living with eyes focused outward is sweet as Isaiah says in verse 11: "You will be like a well-watered garden, like a spring whose waters never fail."[5] And that's the life I want to live. And that's the beauty of this liquid methodology. You can step into any situation, see what is needed, and then meet that need. Sometimes it's as simple as providing a small meal, or just speaking words of encouragement, or maybe praying for someone. And as you exercise this faith muscle, you will find ways to meet greater and greater needs, for a greater and greater number of people.

Let me tell you a story. As I have said multiple times in the pages of this book, I have a deep love and brokenness for orphans around the world—especially those orphans in China. About a decade ago, I had a day that ruined me for the ordinary. The ordinary life that I lived in Eastern Washington would be forever ruined because God showed me someone that day. He allowed me to see something so profound, and so devastating, that I knew my heart would never be the same. As I woke that morning, I knew we were heading to a few government orphanages dotted around

Eastern China. With each of our three daughters who we adopted from China, we had small glimpses into each of their orphanages. The conditions were quite varied, the ratio of nannies to children was vast, and the physical conditions were quite different in each. The trip on this specific day reminded me of those experiences. As we approached the first orphanage, I knew this was going to be a difficult morning. In that small town in a rural province, the poverty was highly visible in both the physical conditions of the community and in the people. As we got off the main road, the buildings were quite worn and garbage littered the sides of the road. The small stream that ran alongside the road was a mixture of greens and browns yet a few people still had their fishing poles out trying to catch something to eat. The condition of this orphanage was not much better. It was three, one-story buildings that were each about 500 square feet. As we got out of the van, the four of us were greeted by the orphanage director, who was quite friendly. What I quickly learned was how under-resourced the facility was and how they had to make do with very few supplies and very few staff. Yet at the same time, it was quite evident on our tour that she was quite proud of the work they were doing. The first building was mostly offices and storage for the few supplies they had, while the next two buildings were both filled with children. The cribs were lined up end to end. In each crib, there were two or three babies. These weren't Pottery Barn cribs; they were rusted metal cribs with woven mats lining the bottom. The babies were all lying down with eyes that were either staring off into the distance or closed for a morning nap. With several dozen babies in each room, I found it strange how quiet it was—there was no crying; in fact, there was very little sound. These babies were just lying in the crib staring off in the distance as they had learned their cries would go unanswered. Walking into the final building, as the director showed us each of the children's rooms, I noticed a closet near the door. Since the door was ajar, I poked my head in and saw several stacks of boxes lining the walls. But at the far end of that closet, was the the image that is still permanently etched in my mind. There, in the corner, in a rusty old crib, was a little baby who could not have been more than a month or two old lying unattended and uncared for. It was a long time ago that I first heard of dying rooms, but I never thought I would ever see one. I immediately knew why that baby was there and what the fate of the baby was. The baby was left to die. I stood in the doorway briefly and prayed over that baby knowing that she was no different than our children we brought home from the hospital who just wanted to be held and loved. But this baby was soon going to die.

We climbed back into the van and made our way off to the next orphanage. The two-hour drive felt quite empty as I just couldn't shake the image of that innocent little child who God allowed me to see. The next orphanage was quite the antithesis of the first. The building look like a small castle with brightly painted turrets and large windows to bring in lots of sunlight. The orphanage director met us there and was quite proud of his facility. The first room he showed us was like every other orphanage I've seen, with cribs laid end to end and two or three babies in each one. There was a bit more noise being made by the children and it seemed that the ratio of nannies to babies was a bit better than most. While we were touring, a nanny came up holding a baby that was about twelve months old. She asked the director a question. He turned to us and asked, "Do you think any of you might be able to help us with this child?" We quickly learned that this child had no tongue, and they could not figure out how to feed him now that he was off milk. This little boy was one of the small percentage of boys living in orphanages across China since over 90% of the abandoned children are girls, and the boys who are abandoned typically have severe special needs. The four of us looked at each other and had no idea of how we could help, but I told the director I might have a friend who knows. There was an urgency in the director's voice because he knew this child would die soon without some help, yet he did not have many resources or connections to get the help this child needed. As we climbed in the van to leave, we all knew this child needed immediate help. His body weight was extremely low and we could tell there were severe issues from a lack of nutrition.

After a late lunch, we made our way to the final orphanage of the day. This building seemed more like an office building than an orphanage, but it was not too surprising since our first daughter came from an orphanage that was also in an office building. The woman who was the orphanage director here didn't seem too excited we were visiting, but she felt obligated to give us a tour because someone in the government system probably told her to. And this orphanage was the same thing—cribs laid end to end with multiple kids in each one. It was feeding time for the children, and they were all prop fed, meaning the bottles were set up against a pillow for the baby to drink. No babies were held; no babies were rocked; but they all were fed. Like the previous orphanage, a nanny brought a child up to the director who, in turn, asked us a question of how we could help. The nanny undid the onesie and the diaper and showed us the issue. I've never seen an exposed bladder before, but quickly learned that this child was six weeks old, the skin around her bladder was red looking like it was infected, and the small bladder was on the outside of her stomach. I asked the doctor if there was surgery to repair it, and the words of her response are still easy to retrieve several years later: "Of course we will do surgery, but we like to wait until the child is about five years old." I immediately knew why. This child would not see five months old, let alone five years. By waiting, they knew this child would die and would never get the surgery she needed, saving them thousands of dollars.

I didn't have a framework to deal with any of this, and I still don't. I just met three babies who all were going to die on my watch. And all three of these probably had issues that could be treated medically. As I sat in my hotel room crying that night, I asked God why he wanted me to see this hopeless scene. The simple response was that He wanted me to see it so that I could help. I didn't know how best to help but I did know one way. I went to social media and shared the story of each of these three children and pleaded with people to help. To help us save even one. I thought back to Mother Teresa's line, "If you can't feed 100, feed one."[6] As I posted this late at night, I knew people back home were just waking up and the post would be one of the first things they saw on their feed. I went to bed that night grieving over these three children. All night I tossed and turned thinking of my own three Chinese girls, and why these three I just met couldn't find the help they needed and how death was imminent. As I awoke in the morning, I went directly to Facebook to see if anybody responded. There were lots of comments of sadness and, "Oh that's so bad," but no one offered to help... except for one person. I got one response that came in a text message from a woman who said, "Let's help one." That woman was my wife. I had no idea what she had in mind, but I knew her resolve. She said to help the baby with the bladder and get her the surgery she needed, no matter the cost. How she was going to raise the money was beyond me, but I was convinced she would. She was always the one to choose faith over fear and I knew she had great faith. I told our host that we would cover the cost of getting that child the help she needed. I don't know what conversations happened that day between our host and the director of the orphanage, but, by the end of the day, arrangements had been made for the child to get moved to a center in the Beijing area that would get her the help she needed. This center connected with a doctor in Hong Kong who specialized in this kind of surgery. They also arranged for a caretaker to fly over from the U.K. to care for little Ting Ting, someone who would just hold and comfort her with the loving arms that every child needs. When I got home from the trip, my wife was already on the fundraising trail. She had asked multiple people to donate, was invited to speak about it at a women's brunch, and, within several weeks, she had raised the thousands and thousands of dollars needed to get this little girl the surgery that would save her life. I don't want you to imagine something that isn't part of the story though. We don't have a lot of financial resources. We are just a modest, single-income pastor's family, with a church and friends who live the same way. This wasn't a couple of people underwriting the entire process; this was dozens, if not hundreds, of families each giving $20 or $50 or $100 to rescue one little girl they never met, but one God opened their eyes to.

Rather than ending the story there, let me tell you how it played out. Our adoption agency told us if we wanted to adopt that little girl, it could be arranged for her to become ours because of what we did. As we prayed about it, we never felt like she was supposed to be ours, but we sent the word out to a couple of families who had been wanting to adopt. At that season of my life, I was an assistant pastor of a small church, and it was our youth pastor and his wife who ended up adopting Ting Ting. She has had multiple surgeries, but she is a thriving young girl in a loving family. All because God allowed me to see, prompted my heart to respond, and mobilized dozens of people to help. But the point of the story is not to elevate myself. The point of the story is to reveal what it means to see and say yes. We each have Ting Tings in our life who we come across weekly. But do we see them? Like Bartimaeus said, "Lord, I want to see."[7]

After Jesus fed the thousands, he said to the disciples, "Do you have eyes but fail to see, and ears but fail to hear?"[8] This is the challenge we face as followers of Christ. Daily we need to see those around us and be an ambassador of the Gospel to them. This isn't just for mission trips or when we feel like it, this is a lifestyle we need to embrace and one that permeates everything we do. This liquid methodology is not a faucet that we turn on and off—it's a fountain that constantly runs and spills over. And this fountain is critical to being a disciple and making disciples. I know we have all seen those people in our circles whose fountains run full. Somewhere along the line they made that decision to see those around them and get engaged.

Having a next step is important in living this out because this heart attitude doesn't just magically happen. It takes work and consistency. As you see God using you, this will become a habit and a regular part of who you are. So how do you start? Start by praying daily that God will put people in front of you throughout the day and give you the eyes to see them. As you go through your day, remind yourself constantly to see who is around you. Rather than going through the self-checkout lines to save a few minutes, talk to the clerks at the store. Go to the same coffee shop and get to know the barista. At work, don't let the task cause you not to have the conversation with your co-workers. When you pick up kids at schools, talk to the other moms and dads. At your kids' games, sit next to other families and engage them in conversations beyond the score of the game. It's not too difficult. And then, look for the impromptu opportunities to interact with people, encourage people, serve people, and love them right where they are. So often we want our lives to be marked by efficiency and how many tasks we completed. Instead, let your lives be marked by relationships and how many people you engaged with. I would guess my struggle is no different than most of yours. When people ask how I am doing, the word that often escapes my lips is "Busy." And that busyness is always centered on tasks and to-do lists. I can't imagine that Jesus woke up in the morning and checked his phone to see what his schedule was. I would guess he just saw those in front of him and engaged with them. That's how I want to intentionally live...to see those in front of me. As Helen Keller said, "The only thing worse than being blind is having sight but no vision."

And that's Kung Fu Theology.

Chapter 8
Discussion Questions

1. If Jesus asked you the same question he asked James, John, and Bartimaeus, "What do you want me to do for you?", how would you answer it?

2. As you look back on the last year or two, what is a missed opportunity you had where you were either too busy or just 'walked on by'?

3. What is your greatest obstacle or reason for not engaging with the people you see?

4. What is one simple adjustment you can make in your weekly routine to engage with people more?

5. What is a need you see in your area that causes your heart to leap in wanting to be involved? What is a step you can take in getting involved?

CHAPTER 9

Word and Deed

"Do not merely listen to the word, and so deceive yourselves. Do what it says."
James 1:22

"Words lead to deeds, they prepare the soul, make it ready, and move it to tenderness."
Mother Teresa

In the past twenty years, the most misused and misunderstood quote may well be from Saint Francis of Assisi. According to tradition he said, "Preach the Gospel at all times, and if necessary use words."[1] Because the next step of liquid methodology is engaging people in both word and deed, the question is what to do in that moment when you are face to face with someone. Often people will default back to St. Francis and land on the idea that just showing love is enough. But, "There is no evidence that St. Francis actually said this...and he was not afraid to preach the Gospel verbally to others."[2] I love how *Christianity Today* responds to St. Francis's quote: "The phrase has again become popularized among the Insta-quote generation, who love the fact that it a)sounds cool and b)possibly prevents us ever having to have awkward evangelistic conversations."[3] People have bought into this idea and have made it a personal mantra. So as we look at engaging people, the two big questions are: how do you do it, and how does liquid methodology stay true to Scripture?

Let's take a look at what the Bible says about word and deed. Paul writes in Romans 10, "Everyone who calls on the name of the Lord will be saved.' How, then, can they call on the one they have not believed in? And how can they believe in the one of whom they have not heard? And how can they hear without someone preaching to them? And how can anyone preach unless they are sent? As it is written: 'How beautiful are the feet of those who bring good news!'"[4]

Paul is not saying just preach with actions in this passage. He is being very clear to preach with words and present the gospel to everyone. He says to proclaim the gospel message to everyone, but we need to do it in a manner where people will listen and receive it. So let's turn the clock back a bit to see at how Jesus did it, because adopting Jesus' methods is as critical as adopting His mission. I love how Pastor Brandon Cox describes it, "His (Jesus) message wasn't motivational flash. It wasn't self-help gibberish or mystical, pithy sayings. It was good news, but there was a call to action. Specifically, there was a call to repentance based on the good news. Jesus expected his listeners to consider changing their minds about God, about sin, about themselves, and about their way of life. He called them into a radical commitment to believe and trust in him. When we simply preach good things without any call to repentance, we make the good news seem a little too good. Don't change. Just stay where you are and God will overlook the deep brokenness within you."[5]

Jesus was unapologetic about his message and very clear about the call to repentance. But his delivery of the message is what we need to examine. A wise place to start is to go to the story of the rich young ruler to understand the heart of Jesus in how he engages people. In Mark 10, a young man came to Jesus and asked him what he must do to inherit eternal life. Jesus reminded him of the Ten Commandments and the young man said that he had kept all of those. Then Jesus responded in a way that our own responses need to be marinated in. After the man said this, "Jesus looked at him and loved him."[6] And then he tells him to go sell everything and give to the poor. Can you picture the scene in your mind? Jesus was in Judea. People were bringing their little children for him to place his hands on them, and he took them in his arms and blessed them. Jesus is kind. He is compassionate. He is gentle. Then as he started on his way from there, this young man came to him. And Jesus treated him just as he had treated the young children—he looked at him and loved him, and then he told him great truth.

This is probably where the contemporary cultural breakdown happens. When I was a teacher, once a year an older man would stand on the sidewalk outside the school with a sign telling kids they were going to hell, and through his microphone he would condemn them. For 2,000 kids, this may have been their introduction to the Gospel and their view of a vicious judge who sits on his throne, and they want nothing to do with it. Love was not evident on the sidewalk. But I've also seen preachers on the stage and the television that do the same thing, in just a less aggressive version. I honestly don't know if they love the people they are speaking to. I hope they do, but I honestly just don't know.

And that's where the balance needs to come. We are called to preach the word, but we are also called to love people—to be doers of the word and care for people. Let me pose a question to you. If you lived in a different country and were sent to where you now live as a missionary, what would you do to reach people? My current lead pastor, Dan, asks me this question frequently for me to process what we are doing as a church to have an impact in our community. Often we have lived in a place so long we never stop to think prayerfully and strategically how best to interact with the people in the area. Not to sound crass or flippant, but I use the acronym PMS to answer Dan's question. First, I would pray. I would pray just what the previous chapter discussed—to see what the need is and who is in need. Second, I would meet people...as many people as possible. I would try to learn their names, find something we have in common, and see a way for our lives to intersect. Finally, I would serve people. I love how Young Life puts it: "Win the right to be heard."[7] Often I see people use words first, and then determine how to serve them. But, instead, we should serve them in order to share with them.

One of our international ministry partners strikes a really good balance of word and deed. Ronald is a pastor in western Uganda at a church that is quite large but also has a lot of tangible, felt needs. The unemployment numbers in that area are near 80%, medical care is extremely limited, and there are lots of broken homes due to poverty, illness, and drug use. Ronald is an incredible leader who has a very holistic method of community development and has invited our church to be part of the process. On the word side of the spectrum, Ronald has intentionally trained men and women in best practices of relational discipleship and challenged them to reach their circles in the community. A a result, dozens of small groups have started, and as of this writing, thirty-two churches have been planted. Ronald also is very clear about the gospel presentation. I have been with him as he has shared from the pulpit; I've seen him share in the local coffee shop; and I've seen him share out of his van window as he pulls alongside someone walking down the road. And in all these situations, it is evident that Ronald loves these people. He speaks with such a gentleness to them, and he is able to quickly create bridges with people he has never met.

On the deed side, the task in front of him is huge. He has about 100 widows and 800 orphans in his church, in addition to an endless stream of other needs. In our partnership, we have worked together to determine how to meet these needs. The tendency as Americans is to just throw money at the needs, but it is much more involved than that. How do we meet the needs relationally? How do we use Jesus's methods to accomplish Jesus's mission? One of my favorite phrases I like to say when thinking about these questions is, "We are the church. We need to do it in a way that Bill Gates can't." Over the past five years, we have seen God move the hearts of lots of people to get involved. And we started simply. Ronald had created a system where each of the widows took in 5-15 orphan children so they had some semblance of a home. But food and water was the most critical need as these widows had no land, and they were walking 3-5 miles to get water from contaminated ponds. We helped them purchase an eleven-acre tract of land, built a fence around it to protect the crops, and put in a well for clean water. The women each farmed a small portion and within months they were self-sufficient in their food. The next need we wanted to meet was encouragement. In the past, we had put together shoeboxes for Operation Christmas Child, but we took a year off and did drawstring backpacks that were filled with clothes, soccer balls, school supplies, and toiletries for 1,200 kids. Though shipping was a nightmare, God provided a way for every child in their church—orphan or not—to receive a gift. Although we provided the gift, it was Ronald's church who handed them out and the kids still probably have no idea how they got there. On top of that, the church provided a meal for the children. It may not seem that significant, but for most of the children, it is the only time of the year they will eat a meal that has meat. Think about that for a moment—a five-year-old child receiving the only gift they may have ever received, along with a meal that is equally important.

As the needs were being met, Ronald was seeing meaningful spiritual growth in the people. Several of the widows were now leaders in the church, kids were getting healthier, and there was hope that was infectious and new people were coming to the church to receive living water.

The next need we felt led to tackle was housing. Ronald showed me a photo with a typical home of one of the widows. It was a mud hut, with mud floors, that remained mostly wet due to the regular rainfall. Because there was only a piece of fabric across the doorway, many of these women have been assaulted and raped. He told me for $3,000 we could build a brick home with three rooms, a concrete floor, a metal roof, and locking doors and windows. And we committed to building one. Honestly, I didn't think much more about it, or the fact that dozens of others did not get a home, until a year later. I was in Uganda with Ronald driving down a local dirt road to go look at a piece of property. "See that house?" Ronald asked. "That's the house your church provided for a widow in our church." Ronald didn't hesitate stopping when I asked him to, and we did the quick tour of the small three-room house. On trips like this, my wife always reminds me to take some videos to share with people whose feet may never step on African dirt. Ronald interviewed Christen in a short, three-minute moment that would become life-changing for hundreds of other people. As I stood capturing footage, my eyes were leaking pretty good as Christen expressed her gratefulness to God and the people who provided the house, and she eventually fell to her knees in one of the most genuine acts of humility I have ever seen. After filming, I asked if I could pray for her, and then I hugged her and we got back in our van.

As we continued to our destination, I uploaded the video to Facebook and told a brief story of how this simple act of generosity radically transformed one woman's life. By the time we finished the ten-minute drive back to Ronald's house, six people responded to the post, saying they would each buy a house for another widow. By breakfast the next morning, we were up to eleven. By the following week, after our pastor shared the video from the pulpit, we were up to thirty-four. A large plea was never made. No campaign was created. We just shared the impact of what doing one act of kindness does to transform a family. As of today, we have purchased and built eighty-four houses. Ronald's vision was never to build houses. His vision was to preach the Gospel, love people, and mobilize them to meet one another's needs. Just on a side note, if you would like to see the original video from Uganda, go to my website at www.kungfutheology.com and there is a link to my YouTube channel. As much as I love this project we are involved in, I know this isn't the only need in the world. But it was the need that God allowed us to see...and to respond to. In light of this, others have asked to get involved or respond to needs in their own area. I love what Mother Teresa said to the reporter who volunteered with her for a week and was perplexed at what to do next. "Find your own Calcutta," she said. And what is your Calcutta? What is your Uganda? What is the need that is bigger than you are that God has introduced to you, and how is God asking you to respond?

This balance of word and deed is critical. It's not an either/or issue; it's a both/and issue. We engage in both word and deed. There is a tendency to think that you must get on an airplane and go to some third-world country to have life-changing encounters. I guess it just seems sexier to say, "I was in the jungles of Africa, or I was canoeing down the Amazon," but the hard work happens right where you live, long before you ever step foot on an airplane to go anywhere. The need may not be fresh water or locking doors, but start looking at addictions, single moms, widows, refugees, at-risk teens, absentee fathers, the lonely, the incarcerated... the list is pretty endless. All you really have to do is open your eyes and see. There's a broken world all around us that is searching for truth, searching for answers, searching for care, and searching for connections. And that's when the church becomes the church. We're not called to be spectators, we're called to be participants in the game. For too long, people have been allowed to just sit on the sidelines observing the paid staff or retired people doing the work of ministry. But that's not what Paul says. He tells the church in Ephesus: "Christ himself gave the apostles, the prophets, the evangelist, the pastors and teachers, to equip his people for works of service, so that the body of Christ may be built up until we all reach unity in the faith and then the knowledge of the son of God and become mature, attaining the whole measure of the fullness of Christ."[8] My job as a pastor is not to do the work of ministry—it's to train the people to do the work of the ministry. That's where the multiplication of faith happens. As we roll into part three of Kung Fu Theology, the route begins to change. We go back to the solid theology we must develop in our faith walk that is unchanging and non-negotiable. We need to believe that God is who he says he is; then we need to surrender ourselves to the work of God; then we learn to walk in the power of the Spirit that God promises; then we learn to embrace and experience brokenness. Those solid theological principles will continue to be the foundation in the framework of all the ministry that we do. As we move from solid theology to liquid methodology, we grow in our desire to be a servant to all, we walk by faith and not fear, we see the need around us, and we finish ministering in word and deed. All those things are liquid. Like Paul said in 1 Corinthians, "I have become all things to all people so that by all possible means I might save some. I do all this for the sake of the gospel, that I might share in its blessings."[9] I think of all the different cultures where I have walked alongside people—the foothills of Tibet, the shores of the Jordan, the hillsides of Costa Rica, and the countless neighborhood streets in Eastern Washington. In each one, the task wasn't to define the mission as the mission, never changes. The task was to identify the method to best reach the people. Where the struggle came was when I tried to make the method unchanging in different cultures. Each culture is unique with its language, its history, its norms, how it communicates with one another, and how the gospel is best heard and received. Sometimes this is an extremely difficult process, and sometimes not so much. But no matter how difficult it is in discovering the best method in communicating the Good News, I know the truth at the end of the story. I know at the end of the story people from every tribe and tongue and nation will be gathered around His throne worshiping Him. And this gives me hope as we strive to reach more and more people with the gospel of Christ and populate heaven.

So many great missionaries have charted the course over the last several hundred years. People like Carey, Townsend, Aylward, Judson, and Elliot have been in all kinds of places and have inspired thousands and thousands of people to further the gospel in unreached and unengaged areas. My favorite is Hudson Taylor. In the middle of the 1800s, Taylor heard the call to go to China. His approach was so unique compared to most missionaries of his generation.

Rather than just raising funds, he prepared for his new life. He went and lived in a poor area of England, slept on the floor, ate simple meals comprised mostly of rice, and grew his hair to look like a Chinese man. He became Chinese to the Chinese. He adopted their culture; he learned their language; he lived their way. As a result, there was great fruit in his ministry. For years, on the corner of my desk at work, I've had a piece of paper with a quote by him. He said, "God's work, done God's way, never lacks God's supply." Not just financial supply, he's talking about the Holy Spirit's ability to work in you and through you. So... Will you let him? Will you let him transform you in such a way that you can walk into any situation and be able to effectively connect with people, regardless of their background, their culture, or their faith?

That's Kung Fu Theology.

Chapter 9
Discussion Questions

1. How have you seen either an ineffective balance of word and deed or an effective one?

2. How do you strike the balance of word and deed? Do you tend to favor one over the other? How can you develop both sharing the word and demonstrating the love of Christ?

3. Where is your Calcutta?

4. If you were sent as a missionary to where you now live, how would you reach your community?

5. How liquid is your methodology in being and making disciples?

Part 3

Expansive Missiology

CHAPTER 10

Go to the Marketplace

"So he reasoned in the synagogue with both Jews and God-fearing Greeks, as well as in the marketplace day by day with those who happen to be there." Acts 17:17

"It is possible for the most obscure person in a church, with a heart right toward God, to exercise as much power for the evangelization of the world, as it is for those who stand in the most prominent positions." John Mott

I would guess when you picked up this book, you were probably thinking to yourself, "I could really go for some math problems today." Or maybe not...but here we go. As we transition into the third part of Kung Fu Theology, we go from Solid Theology, to Liquid Methodology, to Expansive Missiology. In order to understand this Expansive Missiology, we need to look at some math and understand the current state of the world in terms of followers of Christ. As of this writing, according to Joshua Project, who is probably the foremost experts in analyzing the state of the world in terms of faith, there are approximately 7.93 billion people walking this planet today. Of those, 12%, (or 0.95 billion) are considered Christ-followers and another 20% (or 1.58 billion) are nominal Christians.[1] So for the sake of this illustration, lets say there are 8 billion people in the world and 2.5 billion are Christians. And here is the math I told you about: that means today, there are 5.5 billion people who have not responded to the Gospel.

Lots of great pastors fill our pulpits on Sunday morning, but rather than choosing a Tim Keller, John MacArthur, or Andy Stanley, let's take a man named Nils Swanson. He was the man who discipled me during my days at Washington State University. Since there is a strong Northwest bent to this book, for this math equation, we are going to rent out T-Mobile Park, where the Seattle Mariners play and where I have had decades of disappointment in hopes of a World Series title. Since the capacity is 47,929 people,[2] let's round up to 50,000. Tonight, Nils is going to preach to 50,000 non-Christians and every single one of them comes to saving faith in Christ. Because there was such a great response, we rent out the stadium for the next night and bring in a different 50,000 people. Again every one of them comes to Christ. Nils is killing it in his presentation of the Gospel, and the Spirit is convicting people and drawing people to Himself. And this happens over, and over, and over, and over—each night 50,000 people come to faith. So here's your math problem: At this rate, how long will it take to reach all 5.5 billion people?

If I had a Jeopardy soundtrack, I would play it here while you think through this. At 50,000 people each day, it would take 301 years to reach everyone. That's how big this number is that we are tasked to reach. 301 years! If we started several decades before the Revolutionary War, we would finally reach everyone. But, if Nils would reach one person, and spend a year discipling him, and then the next year the two of them went out, and the following year the four of them went out, doubling each year, how long would it take to reach 5.5 billion people? With this model, it would take just over 32 years. And each person would have been discipled for a year. It sounds incredible that, in our lifetime, we could see every person on the planet have a chance to respond to the Gospel.

The last words Jesus spoke to his followers before he ascended to heaven in Acts 1:8 were, "You will be my witnesses in Jerusalem, and in all Judea and Samaria, and to the ends of the earth." This charge to preach the Gospel and make disciples is not just for Nils. It's for me...and it's for you. So what if the church took this seriously and each one reached one? And then spent a year discipling that person? And the next year they both went out? This one is pretty simple math. One billion go out the first year; 2 billion go out the second year; four billion the next. By the time my freshman daughter in college starts her senior year, the entire world will have been reached. Now that is expansive, and that's the method that Jesus uses to reach the world. However, in 2,000 years, 26%, or 2 billion, of the people on this planet still have not even heard the Gospel.[3] But Coca-Cola, whose initial vision was a can of coke in the hands of every person on the planet, is recognized by over 94% of the world—in just over 100 years.[4] In 100 years Coke has done something that the church hasn't—reached the world.

What does all of this have to do with Kung Fu Theology? Well...everything. The goal is to challenge people to know what they believe, and then live it out, and then see a significant expansive movement in reaching more and more people with the Gospel. We discussed why you do it and how you do it, but now is the idea of where you do it.

Before we move forward, I want you to pause from reading on and take a few minutes and consider the enormity of the task that we have before us—5.5 billion people who are headed to a Christ-less eternity. Would you take a few minutes and pray? Pray that God would raise up workers because the harvest is ripe. And take a minute to pray about what He would have you do to be part of reaching the world for Him.

....

In Luke 10, Jesus sent out the 72. Luke writes: "After this the Lord appointed 72 others and sent them two by two ahead of him to every town and place where he was about to go. He told them, 'The harvest is plentiful, but the workers are few. Ask the Lord of the harvest, therefore, to send out workers into his harvest field.'"[5] Jesus sent them to *every* town. If you remember earlier, I mentioned how my current pastor challenges me with the idea if I was a missionary sent to the Spokane Valley, how would I reach it? And that's the question for you. If you were a missionary sent to the town where you live, how would you reach it? Years ago, one would go to the marketplace. The proverbial marketplace today is quite varied as we have to answer the question of where do people congregate or participate on a regular basis? Each state and each country is going to be a bit different, and it is one for you to explore and define. But we can't dismiss it or even ignore it. Instead, we have to be strategic with our time and resources to identify where those gatherings happen and how we can engage with the people there.

Let me tell you a story. Tadeo is one of the church-planting pastors in Uganda whom we have tried to help with the launch of his church in the Kanara village. As he assessed the needs of the community, he found that it is quite remote, physically, from a lot of goods and services, but it's also quite remote spiritually from God. As we met with Tadeo, he said the greatest need was clean water. There was so much disease causing the expected difficulties—constant sickness, premature death, and children missing school. So we provided a water well, but Tadeo did the hard work. The well soon became the marketplace for everybody in the surrounding community. Tadeo literally sat by the well every day, from sunrise to sunset, and shared the Gospel with every person who came to fetch water. It sounds like I am trying to make this a bit sensational for the sake of the story, but he really did do this every day. He did it in the rainy season, and he did it in the heat. Every person in the surrounding 10-kilometer area met Tadeo face to face. Tadeo understood word and deed; he understood seeing the need; he understood serving the community. He did this for an entire year, and the church grew to several hundred. He now has trained up three church planters who are getting ready to plant churches using the same model. We helped these three purchase their wells, but they are doing the hard work in loving the people. Tadeo modeled to them what it means to be a disciple and to make disciples. And today, these other three are living it out— demonstrating what expansive missiology looks like.

Moving to another continent, my friend John, a pastor in Baguio, Philippines, was asked the same question, "Where do people gather and what is the need?" He said water refilling stations are the marketplace in their community. Although surrounded by beautiful beaches and tropical landscapes, the Philippines is restricted to access to clean drinking water. People come on a regular basis to get water from local refilling stations—comparable to the Ugandan water well. As a result, we helped them develop the station, purchase supplies, and they are doing the hard work of being there every day to meet their neighbors and share about living water. This station, "Heaven's Dew," recently opened, and they have already seen fruit of several families starting to attend church. But this station is becoming even more impactful. Just one block down the road from the water station is a local school; 2,500 kids walk right past the station each day coming and going home from school. It's a simple, highly reproducible model of putting a bottle of water into the hands of thousands and sharing about the living water of Jesus.

As we watched our partners create models to reach a lot of people while meeting a need in the marketplace, we began to assess our own community and finding a gap that we could meet. I don't know how familiar you are with Spokane, Washington, but it's a pretty great place to live. We have hot summers, snowy winters, wet springs, and colorful autumns. We have five ski resorts within a two-hour drive and seventy-five lakes within an hour. The outdoor season, from May to October, is warm and comfortable. But once winter and spring set in, people retreat to their homes until the sun peeks out again in a few months. For indoor activities, we have several movie theaters, lots of restaurants, some sporting venues, and a few places to jump on trampolines or throw axes. And not much else. Years ago, every fast food restaurant had an indoor playground where parents could bring their antsy kids for an hour or two to burn off energy, but those have disappeared for a variety of reasons. So we thought... what if? What if we built an indoor playground at our church, created a space to play, and opened our café for families to come? As of this writing, pallets of flooring just showed up as we are just a few weeks from completion. Our sister church in Post Falls, Idaho, Real Life Ministries, built one and has seen hundreds of people start coming to their church as a result of invitations by a whole lot of volunteers. Our hope is that this becomes our well and our water refilling station to engage with people in the marketplace.

We don't want to fall in the trap though of only having an attractional model of ministry where people are expected to come to us. We also want to intentionally pursue going to where people gather and enter their circles and gatherings. Possibly one of the biggest mistakes people make in the church is expecting that guests will darken their doorways without any kind of relational connection. Obviously, that does happen sometimes, usually at Christmas or Easter, but the typical person comes to church in response to an invitation from another person. But without living intentionally, most followers of Christ do not make the invite. According to the Barna Group, only 52% of Christians say they have shared the gospel in the past year.[6] Surprisingly, the most active group in sharing is the millennials with nearly two-thirds of the people having shared their faith. The question continues to be placed in front of us: If the Bible is so clear in the mandate to go share, why don't people do it?

As I wrote earlier, when I started my teaching career, I was very intent on teaching a lot more than Mark Twain and John Steinbeck. I wanted students in my classroom to know that I was a follower of Christ and, at some point during the year, to have at least one spiritual conversation with each individual student. Rogers High School was the first high school I taught in and it was in the poorest zip code of our city; it was honestly quite easy to engage with these kids. But, it took a lot of work. My wife and I were committed to helping with Young Life ministry, for me to coach, and to have our home open for kids to hang out. It really was the marketplace with these kids. Eventually, we wanted to build a bridge between these relationships we had developed and a local church. For a couple of years, we would get two vans and drive around the neighborhoods picking up kids to take them to church on Sunday morning. In a typical week, we would have 10-15 kids with us, sometimes as high as 30, and a few times only one or two. Many of those Sundays we would end at the donut shop with them just talking about life, family, and the person of Jesus. A vast majority of these kids put their faith in Christ during that time, and there was a lot of fruit. But, just like a farmer, it took a lot of plowing and sewing and watering and weeding. I wish there was a short cut in all of these things, but most of the time there isn't. Just like any relationship, there is a lot of time and prayer involved.

It wasn't just the kids who I wanted to invest in either. At every school I taught, I began a staff Bible study as a way to disciple others and reach people. It wasn't highly publicized or anything that we made a big deal of; each person in the study was encouraged to invite others and people came. And these are things any of you can do. It may be at your work place, or in a local coffee shop, or in your own neighborhood, but the goal is to use the methods of Jesus to fulfill the mission of Jesus. As was written in an earlier chapter, we need to be able to see those around us. But the expansive part of this movement happens by going into other people's circles.

Let me tell you another story. As we were in Ronald's van making the five-hour journey from Fort Portal, Uganda back to Entebbe to catch an evening flight, we were about halfway on our journey when our van broke down. At that moment, I literally had no idea where in the world I was. I knew I was in Uganda, but that was about it. We also knew this was going to take a while as the nearest place that may have mechanical help was at least an hour away. There was definitely a cultural and sensory overload as we got out of the van because, within fifteen minutes, we saw a dozen women with bundles of sticks on their head for the evening fire; grown men, either barefoot or with sandals that were falling apart, on rickety old bicycles; buses going way too fast down a single lane highway that had traffic going both directions and also served as a thoroughfare for pedestrians, and bicyclists, and kids, and animals. As we stood there, God brought to my attention a few buildings not more than fifty meters from us. I grabbed my friend Jake, and I told him that we should go see what's going on. The first two buildings were typical, rural Ugandan homes made of bricks with misshapen mortar and no window. The other was a small little building off to the side with a young woman standing in it. As we walked over to her, I realized she was in her late teens and no older than two of my daughters. In her arms was a baby not more than two-months-old who looked quite malnourished. This little building was her storefront, and she had three little bags of garlic cloves. She spoke no English, and I spoke no... no...honestly I had no idea what language they spoke in this area of Uganda. I just knew I didn't speak it. Jake and I both tried to make some charade-based comments talking about how beautiful her baby was. While we were talking, a young man came over and, in his broken English, explained that this woman was his wife and this was their baby, and they were trying to earn money for some medical care for him. Within five or ten minutes of very simple conversations, we had made a friend. He then led Jake and I, and another man who was with us, our lead pastor Dan, into their little village. We met a few dozen people, saw the semblance of their church, and were handed water and fruit. But there was something significant that happened in those minutes. All the barriers they had and we had were taken down. Could we understand each other? Could we relate to each other? The same questions and concerns that we had back home, we were now having alongside a highway in Uganda. Honestly, it's no different there than it is at home. After we finished the tour and the meet-and-greet, we went back to his wife and purchased all the garlic that she had. We gave her way too much money as a way to bless her, but also to give her dignity that she was actually selling something to us. Hopefully, it was enough to get the care for their child. We spent the rest of the time sharing pictures of our families. Our friend Ronald, who spoke this local dialect, came over and was able to encourage them and pray for them. And then we got back in our replacement van and drove off to the airport. We have never heard nor seen them again, but in a sense, that is the purity of going into the marketplace. There was no agenda, there were no prearranged meetings—it was just walking across the street and seeing what God would do.

And it should be the same thing at home. The marketplace is all around us. We don't have to walk too far to find it. We just need to be intentional with it. By no means do I have this down pat, but I try to really practice what I am teaching in this book. One of the long running jokes around our house, and even with my parents, is that I always find somebody to talk to. No matter where I'm at, my kids always say, "Oh Dad's talking to the lady at the cash register, or Dad's talking to the man in the bleachers." On Friday mornings, which is my day off, a lot of times I go to garage sales in my area looking for baseball cards or something that can take up space in my house. Most of the stops though, I end up in brief fifteen-minute conversations with the homeowner that doesn't always turn to spiritual issues, but it always turns to relational issues. It gets to the point where I find one thing that we have in common. Having grown up and spent my entire life in the same town, it's not too hard to find a commonality, and I don't have to look too far to find it. It could be a school they went to, a person they know, an activity they were involved in, but the goal is to find a place where our lives intersect. The reason is, the best ministry always starts with relationship. Even in the classroom when I was teaching, there were a few things I always did to establish and develop relationships. First, I shared about my personal life so they got to know me more as a man and a father than just as a teacher. Second, I tried to find pathways into their lives so I could get to know them and a piece of their heart. The final thing I would always do, and I know there are a lot of educators out there who cringe at this, is I would stand at the door and touch every single person who walked in the room. And at the end of the period, I would stand at the door and touch every single kid as they walked out of the room. There were a lot of high-fives, fist bumps, a pat on the shoulder— things that helped kids feel valued and feel accepted. And it's no different in the marketplace. People want to feel valued. They want to feel like they matter. They want to feel accepted. And as a Christ-follower, shouldn't we be champions of that? It's not easy, but, with regular practice and work, we can all engage in the lives of other people.

After I finished that paragraph, I closed my iPad, threw my iced tea cup away from where I was sitting and writing at Table 26 in Panera, and put this chapter to rest for a couple of days. As I just picked it up, I reread the last few pages I wrote. And here's where my mind goes: "Really? You're going to write a whole chapter for people to read that basically just says, 'Go talk to all the people you come in contact with?' That's what you came up with as the big launch of Expansive Missiology? To go talk to people?"

Yes. It's that simple. It has to start with individual people reaching others. Isn't that what Jesus did? He went to the shore of the lake and talked to some fishermen. He went to the synagogue and talked to people there. He went to the wedding, he went to the well... that's what he did. And that's what we're called to do. Matthew 28 says, "Go into all the world and make disciples."[6] It says for us to go, not for them to come. That's where the attractional model of the church has failed. We're asking people to come to a building, to be with people they really don't know, and possibly don't want to know. Instead, the last words of Jesus are for us to go into the world. To go into the marketplace. Because if each one would reach one, our communities would change. As our communities change, the world will change. I don't know how you're reading this book today, but if this is something you pick up in the morning, then I want to challenge you to take three minutes and ask God to show you people throughout the day for you to interact with. If you are reading this as a group, then by the time you meet next, challenge each other to share at least one story of a person who they had a conversation with and what happened. If you're sitting in your car and listening to this on audio, ask God to show you one person to interact with at the next place you go. Don't wait for the Billy Grahams to go preach to stadiums of people. Don't wait for someone else to get the vision to reach one person. You reach one person. And encourage others to do the same. Just one. Wherever that marketplace is, just one. And that's Kung Fu Theology.

Chapter 10
Discussion Questions

1. Revisit the math problem at the beginning of the chapter. What are your thoughts or convictions in response to this?

2. With well over 5 billion people not following Christ, what do you think are the primary reasons or excuses that people don't evangelize more frequently?

3. Consider your own church. How could you be a catalyst for helping people engage within the community?

4. Where is the marketplace in your community?

5. How can you live intentionally in reaching people in those arenas?

CHAPTER 11

People Farthest Away

"And this gospel of the kingdom will be preached in the whole world as a testimony to all nations, and then the end will come."
Matthew 24:14

"I have but one candle of life to burn, and I would rather burn it out in a land filled with darkness than in a land flooded with light."
John Falconer

Let me tell you a story. I had never heard of Lijiang until my plane landed there. Absolutely beautiful. The foothills of the Himalayas, just south of Tibet, were such a far cry from the smoggy concrete jungles of Beijing and Guangzhou. This was obviously the land where all the China travel documentaries were filmed as the color of the sky and the snow of the mountains provided a sharp contrast to the bamboo that grew at will. The sky was blue. Not the blue one might see hanging over the ocean on a sunny day, but the crisp blue that can only be seen reflecting crystalline snowcapped peaks untouched by human hands. As we drove out of the airport, I knew something was different here. The pace was slow. People drove in straight lines. No one seemed to be in a hurry. The tableau on every street corner was what I always imagined China being. On one was a street vendor prepping some noodles; on another was a group of men playing *Dou Di Zhu* with their deck of cards; and the other was filled with grandmothers leading their grandchildren, each wearing a Hello Kitty backpack, off to kindergarten. The town of Lijiang was also a contrast of the new and the old. The old town was unlike anything I'd ever seen. Wood walkways surrounded streams of water that wound their way through the city. The buildings were all made of wood that looked like they were hand hewn from the Ming dynasty. Whether it was the water wheel churning, or the little kids floating leaves and sticks down the stream, it created a perfect scene that Norman Rockwell would have loved. And the nightlife was just as significant. Karaoke bars and flashing lights gave a modern beat to this ancient village as I watched these Chinese people put their hard day's labor behind them.

I wasn't exactly sure why we were there, but I knew our friend had a plan. He had a deep conviction about finding the most unengaged and unreached people on the planet, and he knew there were some in this region of Yunnan province. The next morning the six of us piled into a van and started driving. Within a few minutes, we were outside of the city and into rural China. Because of the terrain, we were able to see some terracing on the hillsides that looked like they were right out of *National Geographic.*

As we started the drive up the mountainside, the farms became a bit fewer and farther between, and I could tell this was going to be one of those days that exposed one of my basic fears. I hate heights. I don't like standing at the edge of a cliff, and I definitely don't like driving on unmaintained dirt roads that drop off hundreds and hundreds of feet to the side—especially knowing I might encounter a yak pulling a cart in our lane of travel. The road was unnerving, but the sense of adventure was pretty incredible as I really had no idea what we were up to, other than we are going up to a village. I'm guessing we were around 14,000 or 15,000 feet, since I knew Lijiang was about 8000 feet, and we had driven for some time. As we pulled into the village, I had no frame of reference for what I saw. The ancient clothing that the women wore looked the same as what I saw at the museum in Beijing— colorful robes and head dresses. I knew this was an unannounced visit, so I had to make the assumption that this was regular daily clothing. I saw no cars. I saw no power lines. I saw no cell towers or anything that would make me think of modern conveniences. My Chinese friend whom I was with, spoke some type of local dialect, so he was able to have a conversation with them. I'm guessing all the men were out in the fields working as it was only women in our view. The two younger women, about thirty years old, welcomed each one of us, and the grandmother, who was marked by a large black headdress, stood in the distance. As we stood there talking, looking over the incredible landscape, it occurred to me that we possibly could be the first foreigners they had ever met. I have no idea how we got there, and I know I could never retrace those roads. But I also knew I wanted to be in the moment as there was something special that was developing. They led us into a small outbuilding, and the six of us sat on little benches that were probably no more than eight or ten inches off the ground. One of the women started a small fire in the center of the room and put some utensils around it, implying we were invited to lunch. What an incredible opportunity to be welcomed here. She left for a few minutes and came back with half a dozen potatoes and threw them in the fire. She then took a small metal bowl, placed it on top of the coals, and put a few handfuls of vegetables into the pan. And then...and then I saw something I will never forget. The old grandmother came in with an animal leg and started shaving the meat into the pan. And this was no ordinary leg. This thing had to be a few feet long.

I joked with my friend Kyle, "That's a yak leg." When he asked me how I knew, I said, "Because there's a three-legged yak out in the courtyard." I honestly have no idea what animal it was, but I knew we were being honored at that moment and being served something special. As we sat in the smoky hut eating potatoes and...some kind of meat...my Chinese friend began talking with the three women. I didn't have much of an idea what they were talking about but every once a while I would hear the word *'Yesu'* which I knew was Chinese for Jesus. They must've talked for ten or fifteen minutes while we enjoyed our food. When there was a break in the conversation, he turned to us and said, "I was asking them if they knew who this man Jesus was. They have no idea. They don't even have a word for Jesus in their language."

That was the day that my brokenness for world missions became real. I've taught the Perspectives on the World Christian Movement class for 15 years, and I typically teach the lesson about unreached people groups. I know all the data. I know the statistics. I know there are people who have never even heard the word "Jesus" before. But until that moment, in that smoky hut in the foothills of Tibet, with the Naxi people, I had never met one. People really do exist on this planet who have never heard of Jesus before. Let that sink in. In a time where you can be any place on this planet within twenty-four hours, when you can get world news within seconds of it happening, when you can find answers and photos and videos of absolutely anything, there are people on this planet who have never heard the name "Jesus" before. It makes Matthew 24:14 even more urgent: "And this gospel of the kingdom will be preached in the whole world as a testimony to all nations, and then the end will come." This verse isn't talking about geographical nations, the word used is *'panta ta ethne'*—every tribe, tongue, and nation. In short, every unique people group around the globe.

I would guess most of you have some frame of reference for people groups, but let me make sure the playing field is level for every reader. A people group, for the sake of evangelistic purposes is, "The largest group within which the gospel can spread as a discipling or church planting movement without encountering barriers of understanding or acceptance."[1] And you are part of one of the 17,427 people groups defined by Joshua Project.[2] It's amazing that in this age of electronics and technology there are still 7,414 unreached people groups, which is the equivalent of 3.34 billion people. So during the pandemic when people were asking if this is the end of the world, the answer is no. At least according to Matthew 24, it is not. And this is why there should be some sense of urgency to fulfill the Great Commission. Honestly, the work is a bit more daunting than ever before because tucked within unreached people groups are frontier (or unengaged) people groups with virtually no followers of Jesus and no known movements. And on our planet today, there are 4,971 frontier groups, equating to just over 2 billion people. But what's even more amazing is that half of those 2 billion people live in just 38 groups, each with over 10 million people, and almost everyone of them are in the 10/40 window. This window extends from 10 degrees north latitude to 40 degrees north, and from the Atlantic Ocean to the Pacific stretching across China, India, and the entire Middle East and North Africa.

Sitting here in Eastern Washington, it's easy to just put my head down or close my eyes and act like this doesn't apply to me. But obviously it does. It applies to the entire church. And the task is getting more difficult because the places that are left are still remaining because they are tough to reach. Many are very restricted to Christianity, several have great geographical barriers, and others are just remote and difficult to reach. But that doesn't excuse me from living out this Expansive Missiology since Jesus commanded it over and over and over. It's the same call that Isaiah heard thousands of years ago, "Whom shall I send and who will go for us?" And Isaiah said, "Here am I, send me."[3] But you don't even have to leave your home to begin reaching these people. Today, over 1 million international students are in America, and about 75% of those will never step foot inside an American home.[4]

Just in Spokane, to give you a recent example, we had nearly 1,000 students from Saudi Arabia in our city to study. A country that is very restricted to the Gospel sent 1,000 students here. Think about the significance of that for a moment...1,000 young people from one of the most restricted countries in the world. And we just needed the church to be the church. With over 300 churches in our city, we just needed 3 families from each one to say yes to opening their doors. Even more compelling about the church around the world is that there are over 1,000 churches for every remaining unreached people group.[5] What if...what if the church worked together to reach even one?

Numbers like this aren't meant as a rebuke (well... mostly not as a rebuke), but a charge to go and be part of God's work. John Piper may have said it best about how people should respond to the Great Commission, "Go, Send, or Disobey."[6] And that's the heart of Kung Fu Theology—it's not just to work within the paradigms we are comfortable with, but to stretch who we are and what we do, in order that every person on the planet can hear the great news of Jesus.

The command of Jesus to go make disciples of all nations is often misunderstood. Often we just think we are to make converts. But it's so much deeper than that. We are called to make disciples as there are two sides to the coin of discipleship. On one side is the idea of being a disciple, and on the other is the idea of making a disciple. That's what we've tried to walk through with Part One, "Solid Theology," which is foundational in being a disciple. Part Two, "Liquid Methodology," is living out this theology and making disciples. Part Three, "Expansive Missiology," is understanding God's purpose in the world and fulfilling what He has called every Christ-follower to do. I want to share with you the stories of three different people I know, so that you can see how they walked through the steps of Kung Fu Theology and are now reaching those who are far from Christ. These are ordinary people who you would meet at the grocery store and not think twice. But isn't that who Jesus originally called? Twelve ordinary men.

Barry is one of my all-time favorite students I've ever had. When I first met him on the junior varsity baseball team I was coaching, he was just a non-descript, polite young man who worked hard with his very average skills. But Barry was a really nice kid. It was during a weekend of his junior year that I invited him and a friend of his to watch the Power Team—a group of musclemen who do physical feats and then tie it all into a Gospel presentation. Through watching them tear phone books in half and rolling up frying pans, Barry put his faith in Christ that day. Attending a tough high school, Barry's newfound faith was immediately tested, and he moved through the steps of Solid Theology quicker than most. Because of his humble nature, he learned to believe and surrender rapidly while learning that God's power was sufficient to resist the temptation of the world. After Barry graduated, he went into education, which was significant because Barry is Native American and part of the Colville Tribe. And there weren't a lot of Native American Christian teachers who had a burden to return and teach on the reservation. But Barry did. He found a deep brokenness for the students and families there and wanted to give them hope. He easily could have had a more lucrative teaching job, but he wanted to serve people and really did walk by faith and not fear in how God would provide for his growing family. He knew that God called him to this life. It was easy for Barry to see the need as there were many, and a large majority of them already trusted Barry because he was one of them. He learned that teaching there was much more than algebra and U.S. History. He helped kids get school supplies, helped mediate family conflicts, and made sure that each student was prepared to learn. That was Barry's marketplace. It reminds me a lot of the conversation that God had with Moses in Exodus (my paraphrase).

"Moses, what do you have there in your hand?'

(Probably stuttering his answer) "Not much. I just have a stick."

"Well," God said, "I can even use a stick in the hand of a willing person."

We know how the story ends with Moses raising his staff to part the Red Sea, striking the rock to bring water, turning it into a snake, and holding it high in the battle with the Amalekites. It was just a stick that God was able to use. For Barry, when God asked him what was in his hand, he just replied, "My heritage, my love for teaching, and my desire to be used." Simple, yet very profound. And Barry used those to reach his marketplace and allowed his life to be marked by saying a lot of yeses to God and living out Kung Fu Theology.

Tina is woman in our city who I think has done more in our city to single-handedly reach young women from restricted-access countries than any other person. She is another person who I have had a courtside seat to watching her move through all of these steps of Kung Fu Theology. For her, the steps weren't as sequential as Barry's. When I first met Tina at Washington State University, she was already passionate about working with young university students. The liquid methodolgy of her life was already evident as she was fearless in meeting people and had a beautiful gift of seeing people with God's eyes. A handful of years later, when she was confronted with the question of what was in her hand, one answer was that she had a house. Her house wasn't extravagant, but it was the house that every college student wanted—an open door, hot coffee always ready, a chance to hang out, and a place to step away from university life for a few moments. What made her house unique was that it was across the street from Moody Bible Institute Spokane, and just three or four blocks from Gonzaga University (yes, *that* Gonzaga). It was a few years after she got her house that God began to break her heart for international students. And that sense of brokenness was so genuine and real. She began renting out rooms to students, hosting conversation time, and just loving every person who opened her door. The times I found myself there, it seemed I always met a new person from China, Japan, or the Middle East and Tina would always have a story about them as she knew all the students by name. That is such a key to effective ministry in the marketplace and to the ends of the earth—to establish a relationship with each person. In the narratives of the gospel, Jesus did just that—he established relationship. He did it with each of the disciples; he did it with Zacchaeus, and the Samaritan woman, and the rich young man, and Bartimaeus, and the bleeding woman, and Mary Magdalene. With all of them. And Tina did it with Li Yen, and Kyoko, and Aliyah, and hundreds more. Girls all from unreached and unengaged areas of the world, and she did it from her home on Baldwin Street, living out Kung Fu Theology.

The final person I want you to meet is going to get a different name because of the sensitivity of his work.

So, I'll call him Andy, mostly because Andy is a young man I am now discipling and praying that he will have the same heart of this other young man. The incognito Andy is barely out of college and has decided to sell it all and go to the Middle East as a missionary to hopefully see a disciple-making movement among Muslims. The weird thing about Andy is that he is just a normal guy. He's not a linguist. He's not a doctor. He's not an educator. He's just a guy who said, "Here am I, send me." Andy's biggest journey through Kung Fu Theology was in developing solid theology. For him, his theology rested in his head but needed to make a fourteen-inch journey to his heart. He believed that Jesus was who he said he was, but the struggle to surrender his life and come to a place of brokenness was long—not necessarily in chronological years, but in emotional scars and struggles. It was during his years at a university in Tennessee that he met his first Muslim. And then his second, and then his third. It was through these relationships that Andy's heart began to break. It really was the representation of Bob Pierce's quote, "Let my heart be broken by the things that break the heart of God."[7] And Andy's did. And once it did, he was ready to go. I'm always fascinated with those people who don't give a lot of merit to the "What ifs", and "What abouts" or "As soon as," but rather they do what Abram did in Genesis 12:4 after hearing God's call: "So Abram went." Andy is just a young man who is quickly trying to learn the local language and culture, but he has completely embraced the Expansive Missiological view of Kung Fu Theology.

But what about you? The call to preach the gospel to the ends of the earth is quite clear. Hudson Taylor said, "The Great Commission is not an option to be considered, but a command to be obeyed."[8] Just like the Bible calls us to care for the widow and orphan in their distress, I don't think every person is supposed to adopt. But we are all called to care for the orphan. With the spreading of the Gospel, I don't think we are all to pack up and leave, but we are all called to pray, give, and send; and for some of us, to go. What does that look like for you? It might be going on a short-term mission trip. It could be financially supporting someone to go long-term. It could be finding a missionary or an indigenous leader and partnering with them. It could be about intercession and committing to pray for each area of the world. It could be the idea of reverse missions and finding ways to reach people in your own town or neighborhood who have arrived from around the world. Just in reaching Muslims, there are roughly about 3.5 million Muslims in the US (or about 1% of our population).[9] One doesn't have to look far to interact with one of the hundreds of thousands living in New York and California, or even the thousands who live in my secluded area of Eastern Washington. I honestly don't want to soften this for you. God has called each of us to be about the spread of the Gospel. If you get nothing else out of this book, I hope you get that and it moves you.

To wrap up this chapter, don't just let this be data and information that gets forgotten by the end of the day. Instead let it be a call to action. A call to Expansive Missiology. A call to Kung Fu Theology.

Chapter 11
Discussion Questions

1. Is there an area of the world that burdens your heart? What is the state of the Gospel in that country in terms of unreached people?

2. Who do you know that is serving on the international mission field? How can you encourage, serve, and partner with them?

3. This chapter mentions Barry, Tina, and 'Andy.' Who do you know who is living out this idea of Kung Fu Theology?

4. After reading through the information about unreached people groups, what does that stir in you?

5. What is your call to action?

CHAPTER 12

Generational Ministry

"And the things you have heard me say in the presence of many witnesses entrust to reliable people who will also be qualified to teach others. 2 Timothy 2:2

"He is no fool who gives what he cannot keep to gain what he cannot lose." Jim Elliot

1956 was a year that captured what was good about America. Elvis released "Hound Dog," the movie, "The 10 Commandments" was in theaters, Mickey Mantle won the triple crown, and the Ed Sullivan show reigned on television. But 1956 was also the year that the global landscape was changing. Fidel Castro began his regime, Egypt seized the Suez Canal, Khrushchev rose to power, and Israel invaded the Sinai Peninsula. And most importantly, 1956 was the reawakening of the call to global missions because of one man.

Jim Elliot was an ordinary man. He grew up in Oregon, came to Christ at a young age, and felt called to missions to the unengaged. But his calling also came with an undying passion that would consume his single-minded living until he finally found himself in Ecuador wanting to reach the Huaorani Indians, who were known for their savagery and violence to outsiders. But that didn't deter Elliot who took seriously God's call that every tribe, tongue, and nation would hear the gospel, even with the knowledge that it could cost him his life.

By the time that Elliot and four other men, Nate Saint, Roger Youdarian, Ed McCulley, and Pete Fleming, made their way to landing on a sandbar on the Curaray river near the Huaorani tribe, he had married Elisabeth and had their first child. The five men first made multiple trips in a small, yellow Piper plane dropping off gifts to the tribe. They soon felt it was safe to meet face-to-face, and they landed on a sandbar that they affectionately named Palm Beach. After an initial meeting with three people from the tribe, a group of warriors came and speared each man to death, ending the vision to reach the people Jim Elliot had been praying for for years. Though at the time these five martyrs did not reach these people with the gospel, the impact of these men will be felt for generations as it caused a rekindling of the call to missions within the church. Operation Mobilization, whose workers have reached hundreds of millions with the gospel, was launched the following year. Youth With A Mission launched in 1960 sending tens of thousands of young people across the globe. Even the Urbana Conference, where Jim Elliot felt called to missions, nearly doubled in size the year after the massacre.[1]

Five men who were willing to lay down their lives for the Huaorani people, were the impetus of a wave of missionaries who went into some of the darkest areas of the world. But rather than making this a history lesson, it's more important to understand the heart behind this conviction to reach those farthest from Christ and see disciple-making movements happen. Paul wrote to Timothy and said, "And the things you have heard me say in the presence of many witnesses entrust to reliable people who will be qualified to teach others."[2] This is the culmination of Kung Fu Theology. This is what spiritual maturity looks like. And this is what the result of being a disciple and making a disciple looks like. But the goal is not to just reach one, but it is to reach one who will then reach one. Even with churches, the goal is to plant a church that will plant a church that will plant a church. In the West we typically do not see these kinds of movements, but they are common in India, China, and the Middle East. I remember asking my friend in China who leads one of the underground networks there, "How many churches are in your network?" He responded with, "Why are you Americans always concerned about the number? I don't know it. I used to but things moved so quickly and so organically, that I honestly don't think anyone knows the answer to that question." And he's probably right. These house churches multiply constantly by raising up leaders and sending them out to start another church, in another part of the city. It's a bit ironic, but possibly the greatest catalyst for church-planting movements was the Chinese Communist leader Mao Zedong. When he assumed power, he did three things that were significant to the formation of the church. First, he brought a common language, Mandarin, to all of China. A person could literally go anywhere in China and be able to communicate. Second, he built a network of roads throughout the country connecting the remote areas of Xinjiang, Heilongjiang, and Yunnan to all of China. And finally, he broke up congregations and scattered them thinking this would be the demise of the church. Instead, there were cells of Christians all across China who started church planting movements. But the root of this was that leaders took serious Paul's words to "entrust to reliable people who will be qualified to teach others."

So who are you entrusting this to? Who are you raising up to go teach others? I've sat in church small groups where the leader did most of the speaking; he tried to share his knowledge, the conversations were very leader-led, and it was more about him telling us what he had learned about Scripture rather than the people discovering the truths about Scripture. He truly was the sage on the stage instead of the 'guide on the side.' But a good leader should be trying to reproduce himself. My goal in leading my current young adult group is not to be the facilitator for years to come. Instead, I am intentionally seeking out some of the young men and women, spending one-on-one time with them, and challenging them to lead. I give them just enough line where they will have some initial success, but also enough to stretch them and grow them. We then spend time debriefing the process so that the next time, they will continue to grow and improve. I have to think that Jesus used a similar model with his disciples as He was walking from town to town. It's easy to imagine Jesus asking each of them questions about what they saw, what they said, as well as what they saw Him do and say. It's a simple method, but one that is often overlooked.

I find it strange when I ask people who they are discipling and training. Most people can give me a name, but I then follow up with the question, "Does that person know you are discipling them?" This is then followed by some sheepish and quizzical looks. With the couple of people that I am mentoring/discipling/training (whatever word you want to use) I am intentional and ask them if they want to enter this discipling relationship. Because at that point, they are now as invested into the process as much as I am. With these young people, after identifying them, I then try to equip them, and then empower them, and then release them. Again, as I said earlier, it's Paul's words in Ephesians 4 that we are to "equip the saints to do the work of ministry."[3] From my experience, most mature Christians are pretty good at recruiting and equipping, but not so great at empowering, and usually poor at releasing.

Empowering the person you are discipling is critical to the process. I've been in jobs, as I'm sure you have too, where I have not felt empowered at all. I had no voice into decisions or processes, no freedom to create, and I could not strategize about best practices. Whether it was teaching or ministry, in both fields it's definitely not an effective method. And it's the same with the young people I'm discipling. I give them an opportunity to have a voice into direction, vision, and strategy whether it's an evening in a living room, an activity, a ministry opportunity, or a shortterm mission trip. As I empower them, they are then invested in the process and are owning it as much as I am...and usually more.

Releasing the person is usually where the leadership process breaks down. Let me put this in the context of raising my five kids. When they are in my home, there's a sense of safety and control as I am in charge. But those days that I sent them off to YWAM or college, things changed. It was tough because I now had to trust them. Once I came to grips with the fact that they were going to make mistakes, and understood that failures are as formative as successes, the process became meaningful. And the same is true with those we are discipling. If we don't release them, we have become the obstacle in their development. I look back at my journey and the path behind me is littered with failures and missteps of stupid parenting decisions, foolish decisions in the classroom, and unwise leadership decisions in the church. It's just like my athletic history as I look back—throwing four interceptions my senior year to our rival school, hanging a 2-1 curveball to Mike Blowers at the University Washington (is it OK to put in print how much I dislike that school?) that he hit into the parking lot over the left field fence, to 3-putting from six feet out when I was sitting at 88 with my first, and only chance, to break 90. All of those things are formative. And why would I not expect Andy, or Kinzie, or Tim, or Kelsie, or Drew, or Bailey, or Carter to not make mistakes? But as I empower and release them, they are growing in the faith and are each going to be excellent leaders. And actually they already are excellent leaders.

As a church it's no different. We just scale it differently. I've pastored at three different churches as the youth guy, the assistant guy, and now as the missions guy. One church was 200, one 500, and the one I serve at now is about 2,500. The process is the same in all of them; it's just the scalability of each one. The root question is still: how we are recruiting, equipping, empowering, and releasing people to do the work of ministry? Whether it is small group leaders, or serve team leaders, or ministry leaders, we use the same similar process in each. One effective way is, "I do it, we do it, you do it." It's really quite simple. Elementary teachers do it as they explain addition to their students, and we do it in the church. Watch me facilitate a group. Now let's lead together. Now you do it. Whether it is a door greeting team, the coffee team, or kids ministry, the model seems to work as it's intentional, relational, and Biblical.

Let me tell you a story. Every country is filled with contrasts. In China, one could stand in Lijiang in the foothills of Tibet, and could not imagine the acrid smoke of the steel town of Anshan in the northeast. Or one could see the desert from the pyramids of Giza, but the lushness of Alexandria on the delta seems a generation away. Kind of like in my home in Washington State where one drives through Othello thinking they are outside of Phoenix, yet a few hours away, the Olympic Peninsula is possibly the closest thing we have to a rain forest in the states.

The Philippines is the same. Driving through Manila is hectic, humid, and hurried. Literally tens of millions of people are each trying to get somewhere along a maze of streets. Yet a few miles north, Baguio brings the peacefulness and tranquility associated with their culture. The homes there are stacked like the homes along the Amalfi coast, each brightly painted, while a canopy of trees graces every hillside and green space. I love Baguio, and this would be the setting of one of the most profound moments of my life. On a recent trip there, I got to experience the contrast first hand. Our partners in the country told us we were going to do a one day outreach into the most under-resourced area of Baguio City. In a town of 350,000, most of the area was quite similar, except for the sanitary camp area. As we pulled in, it was quite obvious that they needed some help. We hiked up the hillside on a narrow foot path with a sewage-filled creek running on one side of us and a ridiculous number of barking dogs on the other. There haven't been a lot of times in my life where I have felt unsafe, but this was one of them. As the rainy season had just ended and I looked above me on the hillside wondering if a mudslide was going to take us all out. We kept hiking up the hill until we found our host, who lived in a very makeshift home that had seven families with somewhere between twenty-five and thirty children living in it. I sat for a while and listened to story after story from the mothers of how they wanted a better life for their children. Some of them had husbands who had gone overseas to work, and one of them told me the story of how her husband died just a couple of months ago as she held her newborn baby in her arms. After we walked back down the hill, I watched a really unique outreach event happened. Probably 100 kids from the area, as well as many of their mothers, gathered together and the young people from the local church ran the entire event. The pastor, his wife, and myself just sat back and watched. None of us led any games. None of us were the guest speaker. None of us led the music. It was all done by young people who had been trained, empowered, and released to do the work of ministry. As I sat there and watched, I saw our fifteen volunteer leaders hand out flip flops, hug dozens and dozens of kids, and pray over families in a way that wasn't just the fulfillment of Kung Fu Theology. This was a fulfillment of the commands in scripture to train up people to do the work of ministry and to go where the need is.

That night, we sat at Shakey's Pizza in downtown Baguio debriefing the entire day. Having a lot of ministry experiences under my belt sometimes makes days like this a bit less impactful for me personally, but it was so life-giving as each young person described again and again and again what it meant to them to go and do the work of ministry. They shared multiple stories of how they want to do more ministry and how they want to reach their friends. You could just feel the presence of the Spirit in the room as it was such an intimate moment where these young people vulnerably shared how Christ had moved them.

I don't think words, unless written by a contemporary William Shakespeare, will ever do justice to what it's like to walk the muddy footpath in Baguio, the dusty road in the La Chureca dump in Nicaragua, or the overgrown trail connecting the widows houses to their farm fields in western Uganda. Until you have walked those roads for yourself, reading stories like I have shared will always feel like works of fiction. But as I bring others with me to care for the Down Syndrome boy in China, the grieving woman in Egypt, or the trafficked survivor in Thailand, these are the moments that God uses to transform us into His likeness and to transform our hearts into the people he designed us to be—to transform our daily lives into wanting our calendars to be filled with opportunities to engage others around us. And that's what Generational Ministry looks like in a simple form.

Even as I write this, I'm reminded that this is not the way I've always done it. Sometimes as I look back, I needed someone to approach me as Jethro did to Moses in Exodus 18. After watching Moses serve as a judge for the people all day, from morning until evening, Jethro said to Moses, "What you are doing is not good."[4] My flesh side thinks Jethro must be wrong because this is Moses; this is God's man; this is the one who was chosen to lead the people. But Jethro saw that it was not sustainable, and it was not scalable, and it was definitely not reproducible. You probably remember the story—he told Moses to divide the people up into groups of thousands and hundreds and fifties and tens and appoint a trustworthy person over the group. It's the same thing that we are asked to do. Rather than leading all aspects of ministry or taking the responsibility upon ourselves to do all of the work of the ministry, we need to use Jesus' method. For the work to be sustainable and reproducible, it has to be passed on. I know, for me, this hasn't always been easy. I remember my first effort at doing this when I was leading Young Life ministry and decided we were going to do a big hot dog feed for all of the students in after-school activities. Between the football teams, the marching band, the drama production and several other sports, we were anticipating making over 400 hot dogs that day. I gave our newest young leader, (I'll call him Greg to prevent embarrassment in case he ever reads this book) the job of providing ketchup. In my mind, we were going to have four or five large pump bottles knowing the kids would plow through it. Instead, Greg brought one six-ounce bottle of a generic brand ketchup. I was stunned as he set the bottle down, and I actually think he literally had no idea that what he brought was insufficient. It was a great coaching opportunity with Greg, but it was also a pivotal moment in Greg committing to becoming a better leader. In the big picture, it really doesn't matter that 375 kids didn't get ketchup that night. But it really does matter that Greg bought into the vision of our team and our desire to reach that school for Christ. As profound as that was for Greg, even as I write this, I found myself laughing that Greg actually brought six ounces of ketchup to feed 400 kids. But I guess I also once passed out 1,000 invitations to a Young Life meeting that no one showed up to.

Let me finish the story of Jim Elliot that I started the chapter with. Not long after Jim died, his wife Elisabeth, and Nate Saint's wife, Rachel, met a young woman from the tribe who eventually took them to her people. The two wives lived there for many years, eventually leading many of the tribal members to Christ. Jim's vision to reach the people was accomplished, just not in the way he had imagined. I love what Elisabeth said as she reflected on her life, "The deepest things that I have learned in my own life have come from the deepest suffering. And out of the deepest waters and the hottest fires have come the deepest things I know about God."[5]

And that's what Generational Ministry looks like. Passing down the vision and purpose to others who can carry it forward. When we talk about the mission of Jesus, done with the methods of Jesus, this is what He did. He invested in people who would take his message and teach it to others. And for Expansive Missiology to take effect, that is exactly what needs to happen.

"Empty your mind, be formless, shapeless—like water. Now you put water into a cup, it becomes the cup; you put water into a bottle, it becomes the bottle; you put it in a teapot, it becomes the teapot. Now water can flow or it can crash. Be water my friend."[6] Be water. It is my hope through these chapters that you had a chance to reflect on different areas of your life and refine them so that you may experience the richness of a life in Christ, be more effective in reaching others, and have a vision for reaching those far from Christ. And I hope this metaphor that Bruce Lee uses paints a picture that you can relate to, because it is Paul's words that we want to live out: "I have become all things to all men so that by all possible means I might save some. I do all this for the sake of the Gospel, that I may share in its blessings."[7]

In closing, in the movie *Narnia*, there is a scene where Peter is leading Aslan's army in the charge to battle against the White Witch. As he raises his sword, he says to Oreius the Centaur, "Are you with me?" And he replies, "To the death."[8] And hopefully that is your cry too, as we walk this journey of faith. For this life in Christ is worth dying for, whether dying physically or dying to ourself. And my hope and prayer for you is that you will become all things to all people so that by all possible means, you might save some. For that is Kung Fu Theology.

Chapter 12
Discussion Questions

1. In your area of ministry, whether it is pastoring or serving, how are you reproducing yourself and allowing others to engage in the work?

2. Does "entrusting to reliable people" come easy to you? Why or why not?

3. Who was it who invested in you? What did that person do?

4. As you have completed this book, what are one or two of your takeaways?

5. Moving forward, what are one or two of the changes you would like to make to live out some of this training? What does that practically look like on a daily or weekly basis?

Acknowledgements

I am thankful for my family and the prayer support they gave me over the years to take these journeys so that each page of this book could be written with first-hand knowledge.

I am thankful for each of the people who traveled with me over the years and were each a character in writing this book.

I am thankful for each of my international friends who welcomed me, treated me like a brother, and revealed to me the secrets of a life walking with Jesus.

I am thankful to my church, Valley Real Life, and the people, the staff, my team, and our leadership for encouraging me in writing this and pursuing the things of Christ.

And most importantly, I am thankful to Jesus who called me as a 16-year-old to follow Him and take the journey of a lifetime.

About the Author

Steve Allen is the Outreach and Care Team Lead Pastor at Valley Real Life in Spokane, Washington. Being born and raised in Spokane, he married his high school sweetheart, Carrie, and began a career in teaching high school English before pursuing his calling in full-time ministry.

Steve and Carrie have five children who are all walking with the Lord. They have two biological children, Hannah and Jacob, and have adopted three girls from China—Grace, Lily, and Abigail. As of this writing, there are also two sons-in-law, Jason and Johnny, and a first grandchild, Henry.

Steve has spoken around the world multiple times and loves leading trainings for teams and churches across the U.S. and abroad. His missional heart has deep roots and he is passionate about mobilizing people and helping churches find practical ways to fulfill the Great Commission.

Steve is always open to further conversations about faith and the multiple topics you found in this book. You can find all of his contact information at www. kungfutheology.com as well as more information and tools that will be helpful for inspiration, application, and mobilization.

Citations

Chapter 1

1. www.brucelee.com/ podcast-blog/2016/7/20/2-bewater-my-friend
2. Luke 19:1-7
3. James1:22

Chapter 2

1. Hebrews 11:1
2. www.georgemuller.org/quotes/dedication
3. www.compellingtruth.org/George-Mueller.html
4. www.compellingtruth.org/George-Mueller.html
5. 2 Corinthians 12:10
6. James 2:19

Chapter 3

1. https://YouTube.be/R4NlgT65iY
2. Jeremiah 7:23
3. If You Want to Walk on Water You Have to Get Out of the Boat by John Ortberg. Zondervan Publishers 1989 p. 21
4. https://www.goodreads.com/quotes/30608-i-m-alittle-pencil-in-the-hand-of-a-writing
5. Genesis 22:11

6. Exodus 3:4
7. 1 Samuel 3:4
8. Isaiah 6:8
9. https://www.oneforisrael.org/bible-based-teachingfrom-israel/hineni-here-i-am-send-me/
10. Exodus 4:13
11. https://www.thegospelcoalition.org/article/a-pecu-liar-proposal/
12. https://www.sermonindex.net/modules/newbb/viewtopic.php?topic_id=57062&forum=40
13. Luke 14:25-27
14. http://www.songlyrics.com/steve-camp/whatev-
15. er-you-ask-after-god-s-own-heart-album-versionlyrics/
16. https://www.christianbook.com/jesus-continued-spirit-inside-better-beside/j-dgreear/9780310337768/pd/337768
17. Kung Fu theology

Chapter 4

1. 1 Corinthians 9:20-21 paraphrase (own)
2. Romans 1:16
3. Acts 1:8
4. Ephesians 1:19
5. Ephesians 3:20
6. Galatians 5:22

7. 1 Corinthians 12:9
8. 1 Kings 19:12

Chapter 5
1. Ephesians 4:11-15
2. https://www.missionariesoftheworld. org/2012/08/ jonathan-goforth-missionary-to-china.html

Chapter 6
1. Mark 10:43-45
2. John 21:25
3. Philippians 2:3-4
4. 1 Corinthians 5:9-11
5. Ephesians 3:8
6. 1 Timothy 1:15
7. Philippians 3:3-9
8. https://www.epm.org/blog/2018/ Feb/12/olympian-eric-liddell
9. https://haventoday.org/blog/ eric-liddell-after- olympics/
10. Matthew 4:19

Chapter 7
1. 1 Corinthians 9:22
2. https://www.creativebiblestudy.
   com/Blondin- story.html
3. 2 Corinthians 5:7
4. Proverbs 16:9
5. Jeremiah 33:3
6. https://www.churchpop.com/2016/01/16/
   atheist-penn-jillette-christians-evangelize/
7. Joshua 4:5-7
8. Romans 12:1-2
9. Isaiah 30:21

Chapter 8
1. Mark 10:46-52
2. https://www.azlyrics.com/lyrics/
   brandonheath/ givemeyoureyes.html
3. Mark 6:48
4. Isaiah 58:6-9
5. Isaiah 58:11
6. https://www.goodreads.com/quotes/106242-if-
   youcan-t-feed-a-hundred-people-feed-just-one
7. Mark 10:51
8. Mark 8:18
9. Kung Fu theology

Chapter 9
1. https://www.thegospelcoalition.org/article/
factchecker-misquoting-francis-of-assisi/
2. https://focusequip.org/did-francis-
really-saypreach-the-gospel-at-all-
times-and-if-necessaryuse-words/
3. https://www.christiantoday.com/article/
if-necessary-use-words-what-did-francis-
of-assisi-reallysay/112365.htm
4. Romans 10:13-15
5. https://preachitteachit.org/articles/
detail/how-didjesus-preach/
6. Mark 10:21
7. https://younglife.org/about/history/
8. Ephesians 4:11-13
9. 1 Corinthians 9:22-23

Chapter 10
1. https://joshuaproject.net
2. https://www.seattlemarinersstadium.
com/information/
3. https://joshuaproject.net
4. https://brandemic.in/
coca-cola-the-king-of-theglobal-market/
5. Luke 10:2
6. https://www.barna.com/research/
is-evangelism-going-out-of-style/

Chapter 11

1. https://joshuaproject.net/resources/ articles/what_ is_a_people_group
2. https://joshuaproject.net
3. Isaiah 6:8
4. https://clearingcustoms.net/2019/08/18/ international-students-hospitality- and-squishy-statistics/
5. https://www.launchglobal.org/our-heart
6. https://biblicalstrategies.com/tag/john-piper/
7. https://www.goodreads.com/quotes/45537-let-myheart-be-broken-by-the-things-that-break
8. https://harvestuniv.org/the-great-commission-isnot-an-option-to-be-considered/
9. https://worldpopulationreview.com/state-rankings/ muslim-population-by-state

Chapter 12

1. https://en.wikipedia.org/wiki/ Urbana_(conference)#1950s
2. 2 Timothy 2:2
3. Ephesians 4:12
4. Exodus 18:17
5. https://www.goodreads.com/ quotes/9765014-thedeepest-things- that-i-have-learned-in-my-own

6. www.brucelee.com/
   podcast-blog/2016/7/20/2-bewater-my-friend
7. 1 Corinthians 9:22
8. https://www.youtube.com/
   watch?v=OF3PkjLsdvg

Made in United States
Troutdale, OR
04/22/2024

19372748R00137